Babymaking

A
MEMOIR

VINCENTIA
SCHROETER

Helping talented writers publish exceptional books

This is a work of fiction. References to real people, events, establishments, organizations, or locales are intended only to provide a sense of authenticity and are used fictitiously. All other characters, and all incidents and dialogue are drawn from the author's imagination and are not to be construed as real.

Babymaking
Copyright © 2025 Vincentia Schroeter. All rights reserved.

Printed in the United States of America. For information, address
Acorn Publishing, LLC
3943 Irvine Blvd. Ste. 218, Irvine, CA 92602

www.acornpublishingllc.com

Interior design by Nico Seidita
Cover design by Damonza

ISBN-13: 9798885281317 (paperback)
Library of Congress Control Number: 2025906664

I dedicate this book to my daughter who made me a mother and to my mother whose daughter I am proud to be.

Praise for Babymaking

"A poetic, moving, compelling story of a woman's path through infertility toward motherhood. This beautiful book traces the path of one woman's journey from childhood in a large family through seasons of reproductive loss and ultimately, toward a new hope through adoption. The unrelenting barrage of feelings — grief alternating with hope, seasoned with anger and more than a little despair — carried me along, so that those moments of peace, of joy, of succor, were as poignant as if I were living them."

—Leslie Ann Costello, PhD, author of *Helping Mothers, Helping Babies: Somatic Perinatal Psychotherapy*

"Vincentia Schroeter has articulated the path to non-genetic parenthood so beautifully. As a mother thanks to egg donation, I recognized myself and my own difficult journey to parenthood in Vincentia's book. It is a triumph! A must-read for anyone exploring adoption or third-party reproduction."

—Lauren Cross, author of forthcoming memoirs *Mother Nurture* and *Crosses & Noughts*

"*Babymaking* captured my heart in numerous ways. This book is a love story that explores love of family, marital love, maternal love, and love and acceptance of oneself. This is a life journey I was honored to read about."

—Laura L. Engel, author of *You'll Forget This Ever Happened: Secrets, Shame, and Adoption in the 1960s*

Author's Note

The stories in this book reflect the author's recollection of events. Some names have been changed to protect the privacy of those depicted in this memoir.

Prologue

THE RUPTURE

August 1985, San Diego

THE PAIN RIPS through my left side. I'm woozy, trying to keep from fainting. I'm in the hospital cafeteria waiting for surgery. Words float around me. Someone is talking to me—my husband? My eyelids are heavy, but through hazy slits, I can make out two doctors in white coats running toward me. Within seconds, I'm placed in a wheelchair and rushed down a hospital corridor. Every twist and turn hurts my belly like I am riding a bucking bronco. I'm six weeks pregnant. Every thought is on my baby.

As I'm wheeled into the elevator, a bump from the raised metal transition strip jars my insides. We move from the elevator into a white room.

This pain is familiar. I know what's happening to me because it has happened before. My fallopian tube has burst, and I am bleeding internally. I know this means the baby will die. I know this means I could bleed to death.

My pelvic cavity is filling with blood; pain rises up through my body, stabbing my shoulders like knives. A somber team in scrubs moves quickly around me. I shake with cold as they lift my body onto a gurney to prep me for surgery. No one talks to me. Urgent hands snap on green gloves and attach masks. I feel poking and prodding. I smell latex and rubbing alcohol. I am so cold.

I shorten my breath to maintain some control. My brain twists into a fuzzy cloud, and I am grateful because it pushes down my rising terror.

In my imagination, I see a waiter pouring merlot into an oval wine glass. I want him to stop, but he is blank-faced and unmoved. He continues to pour until the glass overflows. The red wine spills onto the white linen tablecloth, flows off the table, and pools onto the floor. I can't do anything. Even though this is my house. Even though this is my body.

A wave of alertness pulls me out of my shivering. Masked faces do not look into my eyes, so my panic rises. I worry they won't care about me.

I grab Steve's arm and say to him, "Tell them I need to know what is going on."

Before they take me away from him, Steve tells the doctors and nurses, "You need to walk her through this and reassure her."

They nod.

He looks at me warmly and squeezes my hand. As they wheel me into the operating room and anesthesia makes me fade, all I can do is surrender and breathe and wonder, *Will I ever be a mother?*

———

I am thirty-five years old, and I want so much to become a mother. I watch babies everywhere and feel excited. There is a chamber in my heart like an unused room in a grand house all set up with shiny wood floors and silver chandeliers for a ball, but no one has come to the dance.

I showed up at the dance at age thirty, somewhat late for childbearing. I grew up in a very big family, and by age eighteen I needed a break from running in a pack of twelve siblings. I'd loved running with the pack, but I wanted a life of my own, outside of house chores and helping with the younger kids. I'd spent my twenties going to college and starting a career.

Then, a hormonal bomb went off inside my body, and once I was married, I desperately longed for a baby. I always knew that someday—later, after school and some career time—I'd want to settle down with the right partner and have a child.

But now, here I was at age thirty-five, pregnant, with complications. In my mind I was asking myself, why am I losing this baby? What did I do wrong? Did I start too late? Wait too long? My mother had babies easily. I thought it would be just as easy for me. What's wrong with my body? Why won't it work like it should? Why is it betraying me? I just want one baby, a baby who will get all my attention. Is that too much to ask? I feel empty, like a deflated balloon that falls to earth. I want to lie on the ground and gently disintegrate into the earth.

There is only one spark that pulls me toward life: my love for Steve.

Chapter One

SPIRITUAL RETREAT

Four years earlier, San Francisco

WHEN I WAS in my twenties, I had many fulfilling relationships with men. My goal then was companionship. But as I got to my late twenties, I felt a shift. I became more interested in looking for a life mate. I was engaged on and off to my boyfriend, Lewis, in a three-year spiral of ups and downs. I wanted it to work, but in the back of my mind, I always saw my parents, walking hand in hand on the beach, talking to each other with respect, solving problems together, and calmly cuddling on the couch. They were my role model for success, and I knew I had not found a match like theirs.

Still, when my dream of making it work with Lewis failed in 1980, when I was thirty years old, I was devastated.

After the breakup, I visited my old roommate, Margaret.

I joined her back at our San Francisco flat on 18th Street and sat at the small kitchen table. She poured us each a glass of Dubonnet red wine and offered me a slice of chocolate cake. I wanted to dive into the dark, gooey chocolate and let it solve all my problems.

"I'm so sorry," she said. "I know you really wanted this to work." On the one hand she sounded empathetic, but on the other hand, she seemed relieved. Margaret always had the feeling Lewis wasn't the right one for me.

I leaned on my elbows and said, "I feel depleted. Like I'm so sick of men and so sick of myself. I'm wiped out emotionally, even spiritually. I just want to hide under a rock and never come out again."

Margaret spoke softly. "You put so much into this. You did everything you could to make it work."

I looked into her green eyes and felt her compassion. I teared up and choked out, "Yeah, I did. What am I going to do now?"

Margaret invited me to move back into her flat and I was grateful.

For the next few months, I felt generally fuzzy, like I'd been dropped on my head. I walked up and down the city streets of the Castro district, trying to inhale some fresh wisdom. But I got nothing. I saw couples holding hands and scoffed, saying under my breath, "That won't last."

I dragged myself to and from work, and at night I hunkered down in my room to watch mindless television to distract me from some vague pain I didn't fully understand.

After three months of this, Margaret knocked on my door. "I'm worried about you."

I looked at her and wanted to say, "Leave me alone and mind your own business." But my chest was collapsed under the weight of my depressed, guilty, and shameful inability to get a grip. I followed Margaret's green eyes as she raised an eyebrow at the piles of clothes strewn all over my bed and at the wastebasket overflowing with candy wrappers.

I didn't like her judging me, but it made me feel more alert, and I decided to take stock of myself. I turned off the tiny TV, lay back on my bed, and stared at the ceiling. She responded to my silence by leaving my room.

Questions I had dodged rose to the surface. Why did I stay so long with Lewis when I knew it wasn't that good? Why couldn't I find a healthy relationship like my parents had? What was wrong with me? I shook my head, worrying I might never find a long-lasting love.

Feeling humbled, scared, and frozen, as if I had hit a wall and there was no way through, I got down on my knees by the side of my bed and prayed the Our Father, ending with: "I feel lost. I need help."

My heavy head dropped into my folded hands. I told God, "I need something. Do I need less of men, less of my love life, and more of me? I don't know. I think what I need is You." I stayed very still, knowing nothing, open to receiving. As if in a dream, I pictured myself walking under a soft blue sky along a wide dirt path of swaying pepper trees. I wondered what this image meant.

The next day, I attended Mass at St. Ignatius Church. After the service, I flipped through pamphlets at the back of the church. One advertised spiritual retreats at the New Camaldoli Hermitage near Esalen in Big Sur.

That night I called and signed up for a four-day silent retreat.

———

I climb into my little yellow Honda and drive south from San Francisco to Big Sur on Highway One that runs along the beautiful Pacific Ocean. As the cityscape gives way to a mountainous coastal road, I smell the giant pine trees and see the curves of sparkling blue waters below me. This land is majestic with its tall redwood trees, steep cliffs, giant mossy rocks, and lush green vegetation. I pass Esalen on my right, with its mineral pools overlooking the ocean. I keep driving.

As I reach the top of a steep curve, I look to my left and see the sign that says, "Camaldolese Monastery." The property is right at the top of the mountain in front of me. My car climbs the few miles of dusty, pebbled trails that wind up and around the mountain and open to a giant deep canyon. I park and turn off the engine of my car that has been humming for hours. As I get out, my ears are still buzzing from the constant drum of the road. I am hit by the contrast of stark quiet this place holds. Can something magic grow in this quiet place?

Though I am awed by the scenery, as I grab my suitcase, my body feels heavy. I am carrying a weight I do not fully understand.

I look to the right and walk on the soft dirt and under the archway toward an A-frame chapel with stained glass windows. I enter a serene space that feels like a library. I look around, smell old leather-bound books and see empty chairs; it's as if people have been sitting in this space in deep thought for decades.

To the left, a brown-robed, middle-aged monk raises his head and smiles at me from the check-in desk. "I am Brother Gabriel," he says. He seems both kind and stern as he welcomes me. He takes my name and explains, "Just so you know, everyone is required to attend morning services at sunrise. Other than that, your time is your own." I am relieved for the time alone, but my breath is shaky. Where am I going to go? What will I find?

"Thank you, Brother Gabriel."

"Let me show you to your room."

He grabs a key, and I follow him as his wooden rosary swings off the belt of his long brown robe. His sandaled feet kick up soft dust. We walk nearby to a plain rectangular building with four doors. He unlocks the door to number three, hands me the keys, and stands at the front. I am taken aback by how barren the room is—just a twin bed with sheets and a dark-olive army blanket, an end table with a lamp, and a small bathroom with toilet, sink, and shower to the side—but I'm also somehow drawn to its simplicity.

"This is fine," I say with admiration as I realize the room

reminds me of the way the nuns and priests lived when I grew up. They lived a simple life dedicated to a spiritual practice.

"Good."

"Ah, when are meals served?"

"We bring your food on a tray three times a day—at 8 a.m., noon, and 6 p.m. We place the tray through the opening in your front door."

I see what looks like a large mail slot and hear a sound of metal as he pulls it open to show me how it works. My eyes grow big, and I feel a chill. No community meals? Uh-oh. Is this too much isolation for me? Will this be more like a prison cell?

Brother Gabriel exits, and I plop onto my hard bed. I look at the plain white ceiling that has a few water stains and tell myself, "Well, you wanted to be alone." A wave of fear passes through me. It is now sinking in that I am truly alone, and I might have to face myself. I exhale in resignation.

I make one last wish before falling asleep: I hope God shows up.

The next morning, I open my door before dawn to the bells beckoning us to the chapel. I sleepily walk behind a woman who pulls a blanket over her clothes to warm her body in the morning fog rising over the ocean below us. She seems too vulnerable, and I shudder. I enter the silent wood-beamed A-frame chapel and kneel in a pew facing the all-glass front wall. I look forward at a stunning view of darkened swaying redwoods still in night robes, towering over the hills below us. Being half-awake makes it easier for me to drop into a spiritual headspace. I float like I am in a dream.

The meditative silence is broken by a sea of brown-robed monks entering in a procession, reverently singing chants in Latin. I raise my head, mesmerized. This brings me back to Sunday Masses from my childhood, where I could daydream to the sounds of Latin words floating in the air. I smile. My spirit is elevated and soothed. The sunrise service sets the tone for the day. I stay lost, floating in prayerful bliss, as I slowly walk the grounds, take in the birds, the vegetation, the ocean air, and note the steep cliffs below me that drop hundreds of feet into a wide canyon.

And then comes the second night.

As I sink into my modest bed, discomfort rises in my chest. I let my mind dive into darker places I tend to avoid. Does God really exist? What if I reach out and He isn't there?

On my third day, I want to sleep in but feel pushed by guilt (in the form of Brother Gabriel's face) to get up when the bells toll. I pull on my hoodie and hurry to the chapel with a shiver. I settle into a wooden pew in the back and take a breath. I listen to the monks chant their prayers while I watch, spellbound, as dawn breaks over the tall pine trees in a revelation of gold and pink.

Back in my room, I pick up the Bible, flip through some pages, hesitate, then leave it behind as I head out for a walk. I figure Bible stories will distract me from really staying in the present with God, whom I am somewhat afraid to be alone with. As I walk, I see birds dart around olive trees. They fly away when I get too close. Step after step, as my breathing deepens, tears arise. I pick a big, inviting rock under a tree and sit down. I am wearing a blanket of discomfort, as if I am supposed to become aware of something just outside my grasp. I allow my mind to open and dance among the trees. I try to communicate with God. Questions pour out.

"What am I doing wrong? What am I missing? Do you exist, or am I making you up? I can feel that I need something more." I drop my head into my hands and sigh. I look up at the tree in front of me and make a demand. "Make a twig bend as a sign you exist."

When I was a kid, I would stare at the statue of Jesus in church, begging it to come to life. If I stared long enough, sometimes it seemed like the statue's hand or face would move a little. Here on this rock in front of this tree, no twig bends for me.

After sitting for a half hour, I make my way to the broad

wondrous view of the mountains and trees above the deep canyon below. The majesty of it all makes me feel so tiny. I walk closer to the edge.

I am nothing, a speck of dust. But my tiny heart is fierce, and I demand to be seen. I reach with my arms, look into the canyon, and scream at the top of my lungs, "Where are you?" And I hear this voice like an echo coming from the far side of the canyon wall. But maybe it is my voice. Still, I am surprised by the answer: "I am inside you *and* beyond you."

Then the most amazing thing happens. As I stand at the mouth of the canyon, looking into its depth, I ask the question I came here for: "What is your will for me?"

And He answers, "For you to know that I am—and everything else you ask you shall receive." I freeze, immobilized by a voice that, this time, I know is not mine. A voice I have never heard before in my life.

I am filled with a stillness and wonder that permeates the canyon, the sky, and my body. His answer echoes in my mind until I repeat it out loud: "For you to know that I am." I shall receive? It seems like He is patiently waiting for me to ask for what I want.

What comes out is, "I want peace of mind, whether my dreams come true or not, and secondly, I want to have a truly loving marriage and from that, have a baby." Saying it out loud cements my determination.

As I walk back to my room, I sing and cry and confide in a God who seems more accessible than ever. I tell Him, "My relationships with men have failed. Was I seeking something from them that I needed from You? How can I grow more in my spirit? Where should I go next?"

Chapter Two

MEETING STEVE

November 1981, Hollister

MY STEPS ARE SLOWER, and they hit the ground in a more solid way since my spiritual retreat. I feel more humble, open, and grateful for God's presence. The day before Thanksgiving, I go home to my parents' house. As I turn the front doorknob to enter, laughter and noisy chatter stream from the bedrooms, kitchen, and living room. I look to the right as my Dad gets out of his easy chair to welcome my friend Carole and me with a cheerful hug. People get off the couch and pour in from other rooms to greet us. I feel excited looking into all these pairs of loving eyes as I slowly inhale the warm smell of garlic, onions, and tomato sauce as it surfs through the room on a wave from the kitchen. We enter the kitchen to find Mom in her apron, hard at work making gallons of homemade spaghetti sauce for a later dinner. She wipes her hands on her apron, gives us a smile and a hug, and invites us to settle in, walking us to what we call "the dorm." Mom points out which two beds we can use in this sister room that has six beds in a row. Carole and I plop down our overnight bags and zip off to visit with the clan.

My bones feel strong, and my chest puffs up in confidence as I think to myself, "Maybe this is my destiny—this is all I really need—to be satisfied with loving myself and with being supported by a loving family." I inhale this idea and feel content.

The next morning, I strut through the living room, still high on family bonding, when I notice a stranger sitting on the couch. I stop in my tracks. I see a handsome blond man with prominent dark eyebrows, full lips, high cheekbones, and these eyes full of curiosity that brighten the room.

My eyes are magnetically pulled in by his beauty. I am enthralled to watch how lively and engaged he seems as he looks around and takes in the scene of the many people passing through. My heart takes a leap. I see a thin, dark-haired man, another stranger, sitting on a nearby chair. One of them has to be my glamorous best friend Carole's new boyfriend. But which one?

"Please, let her beau be the dark-haired one!" I beg silently to the sky.

I have to know as soon as possible. I dart in and out of rooms, knowing she had said something about dressing to go hiking with these new boys. My heart is pounding as I make eye contact with the blond man. But, if he belongs to her, I will have to suppress my longing before it catches fire. I shake my head and smile to myself. I was just content and high on family "being enough" one minute ago. Now, I'm somersaulting like Alice in Wonderland, tumbling into a new adventure.

I find Carole in a bedroom, pulling on hiking boots, then focusing on the fit of her size-two jeans in the mirror. I try to act casual as I ask, "So, which one is Mike?" as I know that is the name of her date. I wait with bated breath, hoping that her answer might change the trajectory of my life. "Is he the blond or dark-haired man sitting in my parents' living room?" My fingers are crossed behind my back. I put on a neutral face to hide my hope, so she will not see my face sink like melting butter if I get the wrong answer.

"Mike is the dark-haired one."

I subdue my excitement and ask, "Who is the other guy?"

"That is his friend Steve. They are marine biologists, and the three of us are going hiking in the Pinnacles this morning." She fluffs her reddish-blond hair.

My eyes light up as I zip back to the living room, sit on the couch next to Steve, and offer my widest smile. "Hi, I'm Vin. The family calls me Susy."

Steve sits up straighter. "Oh, are you Carole's friend? Wow, this is a big family you have."

"Yup, we love to get together. Are you guys going to the Pinnacles?"

He looks at me with a shy grin. "Yes, that's right. I'm really looking forward to it. I've never been to the volcanic caves before. I'm really curious about how the earthquakes created the caves."

I listen to him, loving his interest in the caves, and am wildly attracted to him. My eyes zoom in on his tan face above a well-trimmed, thick brown beard. I watch his eyes light up and get pulled into staring at his lips talk around a perfect row of big white teeth. It is more than his good looks. I've been around enough to know, at age thirty, what a good guy sounds like—shades of kind, thoughtful, and humble tumble from his being. I check off the qualities of what I want, and he is passing with flying colors in the first few minutes. Inside my body, excitement builds. I take a breath. All I know is that he seems like a very interesting man, and I want to get to know him better. How can I make that happen? When I want something, or someone, I tend to go for it, sometimes too impulsively, but this feels different. My heart wants to jump out of my chest. I want to invite myself along but don't know how. I just know I can't let him walk out that door without me.

I lean forward a bit. "Oh, the caves are dark and drippy and fascinating. I led some younger kids through them on a camp outing ten years ago."

He nods happily. Silence. He seems shy. Is he reluctant to invite me? He could be married, I don't know. Who is going to make the first move? I get impatient, another common trait of mine, so it's time to go for it.

Before I know what has happened, I ask, "Do you mind if I come with you guys today?"

He seems to sit up straighter, nods, and smiles, telling me they are leaving in five minutes.

I run through the house, wild-eyed, grabbing sisters by the shoulders and asking if they have any hiking boots I can wear. Each sister shakes her head no. My time is running out.

One sister says, "Yvonne across the street has boots."

"Please go ask her," I beg with sad eyes and praying hands, and one sister flies across the street. One minute later, Yvonne comes through the front door, boots under one arm. I quickly grab the brown boots with a thankful smile, pull them on, and lace them up, fearful I will be left behind. Bounding out the front door, I see a dented, faded-beige, rusty old van with the side door slid open. I guess this is a work van as these guys are marine biologists who spend time in the field. Carole and Mike sit in the proper front seat, and Steve waits for me to climb into the back with him.

I climb up and look around. There is no back seat, just an empty, rusty, stripped hull. I notice one unbolted bench on one wall and an overturned plastic white bucket that smells like salty fish and the ocean. This makes me pause. Will these be our seats? I am taken aback for a second. Then, Mike starts the loud engine, and my spirit feels ready for this escapade.

It rains softly but consistently as this bucket of bolts twists through the rolling hills of Hollister. Steve and I chat shyly about our lives as we balance tentatively on our unstable perches.

"Your family is so big, people in and out, buzzing all around."

"Yeah, we love it, but it can be a bit much for others." We look out the window as the van climbs higher.

"Oh, I found it a little overwhelming and amazing."

"Yeah, I saw that on your face when I first saw you."

I look out the window as we leave the rolling hills behind and start on a mountain path.

We stay silent for a moment, but somehow I sense a cone of safety in the space between us.

Then, he asks, "How is your life going?"

He really seems to care and want to hear an honest answer.

"I think everything is good, really good. I love my career."

His eyes drop a little.

"What about you?" I ask, letting him know it's okay to tell me the truth.

"Well actually, my life is in a bit of an uproar." He looks out the window.

I don't want to pry though I'm dying to ask why.

"I guess you could say I'm concerned where things are going for me."

He seems so vulnerable yet contained. We must use our hands to hold onto the shaking bucket seats as the van climbs higher up the mountain. I secretly stare at his pleasant face.

Did he mean his work life? His love life? I want to ask if he is married, but instead, I offer up a supportive smile and say, "I'm so sorry. I hope things get better for you soon."

He holds my gaze as the van pulls into the parking lot that overlooks the Rocky Mountains. I look back at him. This moment could freeze, and I could stay here forever. A delicious, warm hope brews in my chest. I am intrigued by the fact that he could share his worries and hopes during our first talk.

Our van is shaky, our seats are shaky, the weather is shaky, but as we leave the van, the mountain looks inviting, and the ground feels solid beneath my feet.

Quivering with excitement, I am a chatterbox in a blue rain jacket as rain pelts us on the two-mile walk to the caves. I follow

Mike and Carole toward the narrow mouth of the entrance to the caves. I turn sideways and duck down as I enter. Steve follows me. My skin feels cool as my eyes adjust to the dark and I smell the wet, damp, volcanic rocks. There is something mysterious in the promise of unknown paths. I grab a rail to walk on uneven, slippery ground as rain drips through sunlit cracks in the giant boulders. As we climb up the path, I look down over the railing at a deep pool of water reflecting the jagged spires. The viridian colors—turquoise and dark green—swirl together below the blue-black shiny wet stone walls.

Steve stands next to me, awestruck by the view. I ask him what drew him to biology.

"I was in third grade, playing in a park. I squatted down by this mud puddle. I could see stuff in there. Little bugs, clear water, little plants. And I realized that there is a whole universe in this little mud puddle. I remember I was wearing black galoshes, and I felt this crystal clarity in my body. This sense of wonder about the natural world filled me with awe."

As he speaks, I can see the young boy in him intrigued with nature, and I like him even more. We continue up and down shiny smooth rocks with tall and short carved-out walls of beige and brown, until we come to a narrow opening that we must travel through on hands and knees. Steve leads the way, crawling through the tunnel. I follow behind him and steal a glance that reveals his well-toned body in fitted blue jeans and a white fisherman sweater. I sigh.

Emerging from the narrow tunnel, we stand tall again, and I walk beside him.

"Why did you choose marine biology as a profession out of all the natural sciences?"

"I had this epiphany when I was visiting my Uncle Walt when I was a teenager. We went snorkeling in the inner tidal, when I saw all these purple sea urchins. It was a carpet of lavender that I found fantastically beautiful."

His eyes glaze over with reverence as he continues to speak.

"I dove toward them and got lost watching the urchins crawling on the macrocystis."

"What is that?"

"Giant kelp. The urchins feed on the kelp. I felt compelled to learn all about the ecosystem of sea urchins. I later did my doctoral research on them. I love working in the field—diving and working in the reefs and wetlands—as well as doing the statistical analysis for our experiments."

He introduces me to a world I know nothing about. I am disarmed by his brilliance—to be good at both the physical and mental parts of his work impresses me. What else is he good at?

I tilt my head to the side and lean one hand on the rail in the caves to watch him talk. Steve reminds me of a child who discovers a beautiful shell, finds a crab inside, and has to know all about it. My heart smiles. I feel charmed by his passion. His work as a biologist is so different from mine as a psychotherapist, but he loves his work as much as I love mine. I think to myself that this combination could make for a good match. My eyebrows raise as I feel butterflies in my stomach. They fly around in new desire that our stars may align.

As we exit the caves, Steve pauses in the light, looking up and around. His eyes glisten as we stroll back to the car in the rain.

"This riparian vegetation is fascinating," he says.

"Riparian?"

"That means 'by the river.'"

I want to know more and love hearing Steve bring nature to life in a new way for me. This gray, rainy day is turning to technicolor like in a Disney cartoon.

"See this flower? It's fiddleneck—Amsinckia in Latin. Don't get it in your eye. It has oxalic acid crystals." He walks on and I follow, looking to the sides of the trail and asking questions.

"Wow. Okay, what are these trees with the beautiful golden leaves?"

"These are cottonwood trees. Those are manzanita and these are valley oak."

"So pretty. I'm seeing so much more than before."

"Uh huh. Oh, hear that tapping? That's an acorn woodpecker!"

His love of nature makes it come alive in a new way for me, like in a watercolor landscape, where the contrasts between lights and darks reveal the beauty of the subject. And there is some kind of humility. He isn't showing off. He just loves nature and is knowledgeable.

My heart is growing and I feel a new urgency. I hide my anxiety behind a casual tone of voice and clear my throat. I must ask my "make or break" question. I see Carole and Mike gaining on us as they trudge up the trail behind us, and I do not want them to hear me. So, right before we get back to the van, I ask, "So, are you married?"

"No," he replies with a soft smile.

My heart skips a beat, and I feel a new spring in my step of muddy, brown, borrowed hiking boots. Mike drives back on winding wet roads to my parents' house. Our jeans are soaked, and Steve and I shiver in the back of the van.

I let my eyes slowly drink in the contours—the angles and curves of his face and body, now enhanced by what a lovely person he is turning out to be. The rain taps violently on the tinny roof. It gets really cold, and our clattering teeth cut through the verbal warmth. My mind and heart are on fire, but my body is freezing cold. Steve offers to hold me on the floor of the van by curving the front of his body to the back of mine.

It seems as natural as breathing to say yes.

We scoot off our unstable mounts, lie on the metal floor and curl up like spoons. Steve's heat penetrates my cold back, and I feel swirls of excitement and total security lying in his arms. A smile spreads across my face and I close my eyes in serenity.

In a trance, I half-open my eyes as Carole, who is in the front seat, turns her head to look at us. She does a double-take with a look of shock when she sees us entangled in this physical arrangement on the floor. Her face says, "You don't even know each other!"

But I don't care. Somehow, I feel way past that. He is affectionate, he is protective, he is warm, humble, giving, and thoughtful. I feel no need for caution or fear. He reaches out to warm me in the cold rain. I close my eyes and return to the bliss of spooning with Steve. Some kind of trust was born that day.

Back at home, I float on lingering bliss. My mother takes a shine to Steve and tries to get him to stay longer by feeding him. I have my hand on his knee as he eats spaghetti in a rushed way because Mike is ready to leave. I want him to stay longer. But he and Mike have promised to spend Thanksgiving with Mike's relatives in Santa Cruz, forty miles west, so they need to leave soon. Then Steve would go home to Southern California, and I might never see him again.

I begin to feel a heavy sadness in my chest and fear tightens my throat. Before he climbs in the van to leave, Steve hugs me and gives me a warm kiss on the lips. I melt like warm wax. I want to stay glued here forever. He likes me. I like him too. I don't have to think about it. He is easy to be around, and I can be myself with him. He is smart, kind, handsome, affectionate, and caring.

I watch him climb into the front seat of the van. My eyes have stars. I am smitten, and as I wave goodbye, a new resolve bubbles up: Pursue him, whatever may come. I float back into my parents' house with an urgent question knocking against my ribs, like a bird in a cage: Could he be the one?

Chapter Three

CHAIRLIFT

Four months later, Mammoth

I AM SHARING a chairlift at the Mammoth ski resort with Steve's friend Jon, whom I only met yesterday.

"I want to know your intentions toward Steve," he says.

I inhale the chill air as we rise up the white-blanket mountain in order to ski down again. My bones feel warm from skiing, and I feel playful and light. I dangle my ski-booted legs over the snowy white hill below me. But then I look at Jon's earnest face, and there is a heaviness in his manner. I realize he may not be kidding, so I ask, "What do you mean?"

He looks at me seriously. "If you are here just to play, then forget it." He looks passionate and worried. For a split second, I flash that he could push me off the lift into the snow many feet below. I grip the handlebar, feel the weightiness of this moment, and take a breath. I look Jon in the eye and say, "I really care for Steve a lot."

"Well, good because Steve is a wonderful guy. He is the most loyal person I have ever met. I don't want to see him get hurt. He deserves the best, only the best."

Is Jon thinking that I am some out-for-a-casual-fling San Francisco girl? He is checking to see. The loyalty and protectiveness of his friend's heart moves me. Jon doesn't know that Steve and I have already admitted to each other that we are both looking for a mate. So, I feel pretty sure of myself with Steve's heart. I agree he does deserve the best. *I* am the best for him.

Maybe my playfulness is off-putting to Jon, making him think I am not serious. Also, as an Aries, I tend to see what I want and go after it with drive and ambition. It doesn't mean I am cold and superficial—but maybe I come across that way? I am already so sure about Steve but feel a contrast between my heady, confident new love and an aching vulnerability. What if his friends don't like me? Will I lose him? I don't think so. I hope not.

As we reach the top of the mountain, I dismount and see the wide, white vista—a promise of a bright, broad future for me and Steve. I nudge Jon with my shoulder. "I am here for the long run. I will race you down the hill."

Chapter Four

THE PROPOSAL

June 1982, Sacramento

THREE MONTHS after the ski trip, I am in Sacramento for my sister Cefe's wedding weekend. Steve had flown in from San Diego to meet me for the wedding. He parks his rental car in front of the house he grew up in with his parents, who are now divorced, and his three younger brothers.

His Mom Priscilla still lives here, and I feel excited and anxious about meeting her. She tears up when she hugs Steve.

Steve says, "Mom, this is Vinny." Priscilla, or Cilla, is beautiful, tall, thin, and neatly dressed in a pantsuit and cropped gray hair. She looks at me with bright blue eyes and those high cheekbones that Steve has.

She pulls me in for a hug, sits me down on the couch, and says, "Oh, you are so pretty. I've heard all about you from Stevie. Tell me more."

A neighbor comes through. They put on music, and Cilla gets up to dance. I'm smitten. This girl is like me. She will dance anywhere. She likes to paint, sew, and make sculptures. She is lighter and more playful than my serious Mom, and I immediately feel comfortable around her.

"Steve, since I am in the wedding party," I say, "why don't you bring your mother to Cefe's wedding tomorrow as your 'plus one'?"

———

The next day, my sisters and I take turns running out to the street like long-frocked angels to see if my sister Cefe's wedding gown has arrived. It is one hour before the wedding.

"Is it here yet?" Cefe asks. "It was supposed to come yesterday." She starts to cry.

Mom grabs a tissue and tells her, "Don't worry, I'm sure it's on its way."

We all try to hide our panic as we look out the window for the David's Bridal van. As we put the final touches on our own makeup, Mom sees the truck, runs out and grabs the dress, unzipping the long garment bag as she comes back into the dressing room. Cefe zips into the lace gown and looks gorgeous. It's a miracle that it fits perfectly. She dons her mantilla, and we all exhale.

Twenty minutes later, my hair in a braided updo, I walk down the aisle of a charming brick church in Sacramento. I am wearing an off-white, knee length, satin bridesmaid's gown with a red sash and carrying a modest red-and-cream bouquet. As I stride by the flowers that are attached to the ends of the pews, I can feel eyes on me.

But the only eyes I care about are Steve's, and he is sitting toward the front with his mother in her pearl necklace and those blue eyes that look like his. Two of my sisters follow me down the aisle, the three of us in identical gowns and hairdos. As we make it to the altar and turn, I hear the tune "Here Comes the Bride." The guests stand for my sister Cefe's entrance. Escorted by my father, she looks so happy in her long white gown and long mantilla-style lace veil. Dad kisses my beautiful sister on the cheek and relinquishes her to her beaming groom, Dave.

We groomsmen and bridesmaids stand aside as the groom and bride take the center and face the priest at the altar. We turn to face the guests, and I look at Steve. He is wearing a gray suit with a blue-and-gold tie.

I squint to see that his eyes are kind of blue, no, maybe more green?

I feel a tug on my sleeve from my sister Anita. "Vin, Cefe is handing you her bouquet to give to Maria."

I take my eyes off Steve and am back long enough to hand the bridal bouquet from Cefe to Anita to Maria. I make an "oops" face and try to compose myself again.

The priest says, "Marriage is a somber covenant made in the eyes of God." This is not just a wedding ceremony but a High Mass, so it is longer than most masses and involves prayers I've memorized since I was seven along with lots of kneeling and standing. I do it all by rote. "May God bring blessings onto this couple as they vow to love each other for all eternity."

I crane my neck to look at Cefe and Dave, and my heart goes out to them with all my wishes for a long life of love and devotion. But then, my heart gets magnetically pulled away from the altar and back to the second row, three spots in, where I steal glances and smile at Steve from my bridesmaid's perch. Steve winks at me, and I purse my lips to try and act proper, but my eyes are pools of love.

Cilla, a devout Mormon, frowns and elbows Steve to behave. He looks at me and shrugs, and I bite my lip to suppress a smile. His Mom is disarmed as she can't stop our flirting and covers her mouth as she giggles.

I get up from the table I share with Steve and his Mom at the reception hall to dance and laugh with my siblings to Cefe's theme song, "Brick House."

Steve joins us and looks charmed by the family camaraderie. He says, "You guys really enjoy each other's company."

We take a walk outside in the garden and hold hands. I climb up some brick steps to the upper floor as Steve follows me. He asks, "Are you going to look this beautiful at our wedding?"

I freeze with one foot on one step, the other in the air. The words "our wedding" fill my head. I touch my toe to the step, quickly turn on my high-heeled foot, and look at him. I stutter, "Are you, does this mean, uh…"

He looks kind of shocked but also mesmerized. He laughs with the most radiant eyes I have ever seen and says, "Yes, will you marry me?"

I say, "Yes." My blood is thudding with excitement, and my heart floods with love as if my whole world has just lit up in fireworks. We kiss and zip back down the steps. I take Steve's hand, and we run into the reception, where people are eating at their tables. We make a beeline for his mother and tell her first. She gasps and tears up in happiness.

Then we go to my parents' table and whisper our news to them. My mom smiles widely. Dad opens his mouth in surprise. Then his eyes sparkle with joy. He says, "Congratulations" and hops up from his chair.

My father grabs the microphone from the bride's table and taps on it to get everyone's attention. All the guests look up from their tables. "I have an announcement to make."

All my siblings turn and stare at my twenty-two-year-old younger brother Peter, thinking Dad is about to announce his engagement to the woman he has dated for three years. Peter's eyes get big as saucers, and his face flushes as he holds his fork in mid-air, looking trapped.

Dad says, "My daughter Vincentia just got engaged to her boyfriend, Steve."

Peter sighs in relief, and everyone turns their heads toward us and claps.

Cefe and Dave, the bride and groom, are gracious, but Cefe later jokes (and my siblings will side with her), "You stole my thunder at my wedding reception."

———

A few months later, with some fear but mostly excitement, I close my private therapy practice in San Francisco, stuff all my belongings into a small U-Haul, and drive my little yellow Honda eight hours south to San Diego. A year later, in July 1983, Steve and I get married.

———

I am lying in marital bliss in a small cabin on the fifth day of our honeymoon, my heart smiling with contentment. We are in one of Steve's favorite spots, which I have fallen in love with this past week: the red clay sand and orange-yellow striped mountains of Zion National Park. A new longing rises in me as I think about the fact that I am thirty-three and Steve is thirty-six. Neither of us has had children. Steve is so warm and kindhearted; I know he would make a great father.

I turn to him in bed and say, "I want to have a baby."

Steve looks at me confidently and says, "Me too."

"Some people wait a year to get to know each other and have time just as a couple before having children. I don't feel a need for that, do you?"

Steve shakes his head, "No. And I can't wait to bring our child here."

Chapter Five

WICKER CHAIR

Age 33, 1983, Encinitas

ON A WARM SUMMER SATURDAY, I cross the green grass in my flip-flops to swim and lounge at the community pool in our condo complex. It is just a few weeks after our honeymoon, and I have given up birth control.

As I settle into a lounge chair, I look through the gate to the houses across the street. I see a serene, smiling, young pregnant woman, with long, straight brown hair, holding a toddler's hand. She looks both ways, then crosses the street and enters the gate to get to the pool. She drops her gear in a lounge chair, gently carries her toddler in her arms, and they splash in the water.

I have this sensation of glee bubbling to the surface. I want to be just like her. I hope that, soon, I will be carrying our baby. Having a baby with Steve will make our family complete and make my dream come true. I am amazed I've come this far. It wasn't that long ago I was upset about Lewis. What a disaster a life with him would have been. I can't imagine myself there now. No, Steve is my perfect partner, and everything is going perfectly.

Back in my room, I turn my side profile to the mirror, stick out my stomach to look pregnant, and cup my hands under my puffed-out belly. I imitate the serene, calm smile that my mother wore when she was pregnant. She was pregnant during most of my childhood. I picture her wearing an apron stretched over a maternity top, humming while folding dish towels on the kitchen table. I hum a little tune. I can't wait for my turn to be like her.

——————

Three months go by. It is October.

Steve and I are standing at the sink doing breakfast dishes when I elbow him playfully.

"I haven't had my period yet."

"What?"

"Yeah. It's six days late!"

"Really?" He looks at me with excitement in his eyes.

"You know, my period is always on time."

"Wow. This could really be it."

"If I am pregnant, the baby will be born in July!"

"Every time I think of it, I see three of us hiking at Zion National Park."

"Oh, yeah. Three of us. So exciting."

We hug each other. Then, I touch his nose with my soapy finger. He laughs and playfully hits me with the dish towel. My smile drops, and I rub my belly with a touch of fear. Come on, baby.

——————

A few days later, while driving home from work, I feel a cramp in my stomach and step on the gas so I can get home quickly. Thoughts race through my mind. Please, let it be okay. I take a breath while telling myself it's going to be fine and this is probably normal. I park in our carport and open the front door to our house.

Steve turns from reading a book on the couch and says, "Hey, how'd your day go?"

"I can't talk right now," I mumble as I run to the bathroom. I see bright red blood in the toilet. No, oh, no, my period! My head gets spacy. I don't want to believe it. My heart sinks as I flush the toilet and stare as the red liquid twirls, turns to pink, then turns to clear, and disappears. That easily. The first hoped-for pregnancy dream dies. My head feels heavy, and I let it sink into my hands as I shed a tear. Am I one of those women who can't get pregnant right away?

As I exit the bathroom, Steve asks, "What's wrong?"

"My period started." Steve puts his book down and looks at me.

"Oh, no." He frowns. Then, his eyes kind of glaze over. "Are you okay?"

"Yeah. But I wanna be alone for a minute."

I go out the front door and lean against my car. I feel defeated, like I've let us both down. I don't feel loving or love-able right now. We both wanted to try right away, and we did, and it didn't work. It is our four-month wedding anniversary. I sigh and give myself more grace. "You know you are impatient. Let up on yourself. Give it more time."

———

At Christmastime, we drive home to my parents' house where we all gather every year. As my siblings' families grow, the house expands to fit everyone. My baby nephew Trenton nurses as he sits on his mother Cefe's lap. She unwraps and squeezes a squeaky, yellow toy duck. "Look Trenton, for you."

Trenton hears "quack, quack" and turns and giggles.

It is Christmas morning, 1983. Thirty of us have crowded into the living room of my parents' house in our robes to open the mountain of gifts under the tree. We make our way through the mountain, call out names, then watch each other open gifts and create piles of discarded wrapping paper, tissue, and ribbon.

I sit on the edge of the couch and look out the window at my hometown. The two huge elm trees in front of the house sway gently in the morning breeze, and I smell a whiff of almonds and figs from the neighbor's trees next door.

I turn back and take in my big family. Most of us have grown and moved away—and many have started families of their own —but we return home to swell the house with laughter every year.

After the last scrap of giftwrap is cleaned up, my mother looks at my sister Cefe and me and whispers, "Come with me." We follow her into her bedroom. "I just bought this." She points to a toddler's wicker chair painted with colored flowers on the wooden back. One of my twin sisters has two sons, my other twin sister has one, and Cefe has one. So my parents now have four grandchildren, all boys. My mother smiles as she leans down and rocks the little chair with her hand. "I am saving this for my first granddaughter." My face lights up, and my heart jumps with joy, hoping I might become that mother and win that chair.

———

My period mocks me by showing up on time month after month for another four months—December, January, February and March. Blood is like my enemy now, an ill omen, a harbinger of the death of my dream month after month.

One night, I can't fall asleep, so I stare at the clock high up on the dresser. It looks like an angry tyrant, refusing to give me what I want. It keeps ticking, louder and angrier. I know this about me, that when I want something, I get impatient with time going too slowly. I remind myself, "Patience is a virtue—a virtue you don't have." I know it takes some couples longer, but we are ready now. I jump to a future fear. How long will this take? I recently read that the medical world labels you "infertile" after one year of unsuccessful attempts to get pregnant. The word "infertile" makes me cringe.

But time keeps marching to its own drum. We have been trying to get pregnant for nine months, and it is time to find out why we can't conceive. As we turn the knob and enter the Kaiser fertility clinic, I steal glances at couples in green plastic chairs. Are these people with infertility problems? I don't want to be one of these people. We sit, and I pick a magazine for distraction.

A woman gets up from her chair in the waiting room and approaches us. Her face looks pained as she shoves a blue flyer toward us. In the tiniest voice, she says, "I am advertising a support group for infertile couples."

Steve takes the flyer, and both of us ignore it. Steve puts his hand on my knee and looks at me with a face that says, "I don't want this to be us."

A receptionist calls our names, and we head back to meet Dr. Reinsch. He is about fifty years old, has a thick head of dark hair, and is warm and friendly. I see all the photos of babies on the wall behind him. I am kind of jittery and numb, still fighting against the idea that we have a fertility problem.

"Where do these babies come from?" I ask. I feel scared, as I am holding onto wanting our baby from our own bodies but also intrigued by all these photos. I want a baby. Dr. Reinsch makes babies happen. If we have a problem, I hope he can solve it somehow.

"Oh, these are our success stories—making our patients happy parents, whether from natural birth, from IVF, donor sperm, other treatments, or from adoption." I like this answer, as if there are many doors to go through to achieve the baby goal. He asks about us, nods, and offers a speech he's probably given hundreds of times. As I listen to the details, it is an information dump—and a lot to take in—but also promises that there are avenues to pursue.

"We will start with testing; we want to find out where the issue might be. We can do a semen analysis test first."

I look at Steve. Could he be the problem? Somehow, I feel relieved that it might not be me.

Dr. Reinsch continues. "We might do a hysterosalpingogram (HSG) to check the condition of your fallopian tubes and your uterus and look for blockages. If need be, we can do IVF to capture your eggs for fertilization. This requires surgery. You might need shots of Clomid to increase egg production."

I was interested in hearing more about the testing process, but when I heard about "surgery and shots," my mind got hazy, and I drifted away. I have never had surgery. I quiver at the idea of being cut into.

Dr. Reinsch ends the session on a hopeful note. "Keep trying on your own. Remember, it's only been nine months since you started trying. A year is considered infertile, but if you'd like, we can start up the testing next week."

———

The weightiness of reality slows my steps as we walk silently to the parking garage. A part of me still holds out hope that we can do it on our own. Another part of me sees those babies' faces behind the doctor's desk, and I feel grateful that modern medicine is there to help.

The various treatment options swirl above my head as Steve starts the car and says, "Here's what I think. We both know we want a family. If pregnancy doesn't work, we can start looking into adoption."

"I want to try and get pregnant before we consider adoption, but I was not drawn to what he said about donor sperm. I don't want a baby that has half my genes, and half from a stranger. What do you think?"

"I agree. I don't like that either. I'd rather it had no genes of either of ours."

As we drive home, my head fills with all we heard. Some of the treatments involve surgery. I don't want all those problems. I want to push it all away. What's wrong? What if it is me?

Late that night, my mind races like a scared rabbit. Before we fall asleep, I tell Steve about some of my dark thoughts.

"Maybe this means I'm not fertile like my mother because I'm not earthy enough."

"What? Oh, no. I think that is wrong. Is this the idea that you have a limited amount of blessings in your life? Just because you are successful in your career, and you have me, you think you don't also get to have a child?"

"I don't know, but it feels like that sometimes. Like I don't get to have everything I want as a woman."

"That is an anti-feminist statement, isn't it?"

"What? You know I am a feminist. Oh, so you are calling *me* anti-feminist?"

"Well, I think people take what is physiological and attach psychological significance to it because they don't understand."

"Whoa, Steve, now you're explaining psychology to *me*?" I feel a giggle which lightens my mood.

Steve continues. "I know, but the infertility nurse told us that anxiety does not cause infertility. Infertility causes anxiety."

Steve is making sense with his brainy feminist and psychological points, but my emotional brain isn't able to take it in. I bury my head in the pillow but can't sleep. I feel teary as my head begins to spin. I grab my journal and write the following in large letters, filling a whole page:

I feel inadequate, embarrassed,
less feminine. I'm cold, old
like
a
flower
already dying

without
ever
having
bloomed.

———

I wake up the next morning after the doctor's appointment and write a letter to my unborn child, using a name I've been dreaming of using if we have a daughter.

"Dear Marena,

I know you are alive, real, and will be here someday. Maybe I'll even show you this letter. Perhaps you will emerge from the physical union of your parents, Steve and me, or you may come into our loving arms from another couple's physical union.

But you are still our baby—made of our need and want to love and raise you. Yesterday, I learned I may not have an easy time making you join us, and so I feel much pain. I just want you to know that I *already* know you and love you.

I will wait for you. Today I wait for you in pain. I make you more real by this letter. Someday I will wait for you in joyous expectation. I don't know if it will be from a hospital bed in a maternity ward or an adoption agency, but I will be waiting. And Steve, your father, will be waiting. You will be everything we want, yet you will be totally uniquely you. We have so much love between us that we sometimes feel like the luckiest people on earth. We want to share our love with you—a special love— the love of parents.

You are already showing your independence by coming, not when we are ready (which is now) but when you are ready. Maybe that's a lesson for us. And whenever you join us, and wherever you come from (and you do come from God, ulti- mately) it will be the right time.

I feel more calm as I end this. You are sealed in my heart with hope and love."

———

One week later, our tests begin. They take blood from me and semen samples from Steve. Steve's sperm sample is so high, the doctor says he is probably a "super-stud" but might have a rare "polyspermia," which means he has too much sperm. They take a second sperm sample and dismiss the polyspermia possibility. We are frustrated that there are no answers.

The doctor gets specific with us. "Use a basal thermometer to measure your temperature to determine when you are ovulating. Check the viscosity of your mucus. Have sex often in that mid-cycle window."

We follow the rules and have sex religiously, whether we are in the mood or not. We are deeply in love, but sometimes the demanding time machine makes sex mechanical. I write a silly sexual poem to add levity to our task. It starts, "Screw, screw, screw, that's all we ever do . . ."

Time gets absorbed in just this one act, like a sponge soaking up all the water, leaving nothing left. I am so obsessed with intercourse during ovulation and trying to get pregnant that the outside world fades away. I stay in bed after sex with my legs in the air for thirty minutes, so gravity can help move the sperm to the egg. I know that is a crazy old wives' tale, but I'm crazy to try anything.

I lose track of time that is controlled by my cycle and our attempts to get pregnant. Nearly a year flies by.

Then, the fertility clinic calls with a plan. "We want to do a post-coital exam. The test examines the interaction between the sperm and mucus of the cervix."

It feels strange to have these strangers so involved in our lovemaking life, but we are up for anything and decide to take the test. Now, this is during ovulation, so we have been having sex every day for a few days. We get dressed and zip into the car right after sex and drive forty-five minutes to the clinic. I'm still in a happy, druggy afterglow, and now I have to button up and act normal. As we drive, I look out the window and shudder.

Steve looks at me and laughs. "This is weird, right?"

I nod. "Very. It better be worth the weirdness."

At the exam, the nurse-midwife tells me that "everything looks perfect" and adds, "You might be five hours pregnant." A jolt of excitement surges from my pelvis to my throat.

As we drive home, I smile at Steve, and his eyes twinkle as he squeezes my knee. I was buoyed by the possibility that I could be pregnant.

But on July 1, at 6 p.m., my period starts. A full year has now rolled by. A year without a pregnancy. I feel crushed and want to hide under the covers for days.

But Steve wants to go to a party with his work colleagues for the Fourth of July, so I drag myself up, throw on summer clothes, and go with him, thinking maybe the party will get my mind off babies.

Most of the people at the summer party are in their thirties, like us. We walk through the house, nodding at smiling people with drinks in their hands. I try to be cheerful, hoping to shake the heavy sadness I feel. We go out the back door, onto the wooden deck, which looks over the big, leafy backyard full of more cheerful people.

Julie and Alan, work colleagues of Steve's, walk up to me. Julie turns to the side, her belly bulging from her loose dress, and tells me, "I'm nine months along. We are actually due tomorrow." She places her head on her husband Alan's shoulder.

His chest swells as he says, "It's our first child."

Even though I want to be happy for them, the best I can do is offer a stiff smile and nod politely. They are a snapshot of what I want and don't have. The green vapor of jealousy threatens to fill up every cavity in my body, so I turn and grab a drink at the buffet table right behind me. The liquid absorbs the vapor long enough for me to change the subject to keep from falling apart. I have to get away from them.

I find an empty bench in a corner and look over the balcony toward the dots of city lights below.

Linda, another work colleague of Steve's, sits too close to me on my bench, leans in, and asks, "Have you heard my good news?"

"No."

"I'm pregnant."

I tolerated the first couple, as I didn't want to rain on their parade, but I feel trapped on this bench, and my anger rises. I tighten my jaw as Linda babbles on and on, spewing her joy all over me like vomit. I ache to get away from the spray but can't move without looking rude. I peer down into the backyard to find a distraction. But the backyard is bursting with babies and toddlers in red, white, and blue, mocking me by their existence. I feel betrayed, like there is nowhere to hide.

Linda continues, "Are you and Steve planning a family?"

"Ah, yes. We are working on it." My voice shakes. It is like in *The Hobbit* when Bard the Bowman shoots the arrow into the one spot in the flying dragon's body that isn't covered in protective scales. I am wounded and falling through the air. I swallow the large lump in my throat and do somersaults and triple flips inside my body to avoid crying in front of her, this bowman, this woman I barely know. This pregnant woman, another one who has captured the brass ring, the ring I am still reaching for. The green vapor starts filling my body again. I wish I could breathe fire at her. Instead, I give her an insincere smile, stand up, and walk away.

I find Steve. He is enjoying chatting with his work friends, so I give him more time, then whisper, "Please take me home."

———

The doctor is doing yet another new test. I lie on my back and look at the monitor during the HSG. The doctor says, "You can see that the dye has gone through. This means your uterus and fallopian tubes are clear. We see no abnormalities or blockages."

I exhale in relief.

He tells me, "Go home and try for a few more months, but remember to take your temperature with your basal thermometer to be sure you are trying during the peak times of fertility."

I sigh with fatigue. Of course I know this. It feels like I've been doing it forever.

———

A month later, on the August morning of Steve's thirty-ninth birthday, I look over at him and wonder how he feels. I try in my cheeriest voice: "Happy Birthday. What do you want to do today?"

Steve shrugs. "Nothing. I don't know."

Steve doesn't like being in the limelight, so maybe it means nothing, but he sounds depressed. I worry he is getting fatigued with this infertility journey, and maybe with me, because we aren't getting pregnant. Is the mechanical sex making him like me less? I know he is loyal to me. I know he tends to endure things, making him more patient than me, but what is this doing to him?

I write in my journal:

Steve is almost forty without a baby . . . What if I can't have children? Does that scare him, sadden him? Will he get more depressed the longer I remain unpregnant?

Dr. Reinsch calls and says, "We are going to schedule surgery to further examine why you aren't getting pregnant."

Surgery? His words send a ripple of fear through my body. He sounds impatient. I tighten my gut in fear. "Oh, that kind of scares me. I've never had any surgeries."

He pauses and says thoughtfully, "Well, think about it, because otherwise, we have no answers."

I hang up the phone, lie on my bed, and talk to God. Ever since my spiritual retreat, I have felt a closer connection with God. Whenever I doubt His existence, or even His interest in my life, I recall what He said, "For you to know that I am . . ."

I close my eyes, breathe, and feel His presence. I think back to when I was around ten years old. Every night my father would stand in the doorway of "the girls' room," or "the dorm," as it had six beds in a row for us sisters. He would lead us in prayers and I would feel wrapped in a blanket of his love and God's love. After prayers he would admonish us to be quiet and go to sleep. Sometimes, the prayers would help me float like a cloud and drift away to sleep, but other times, my mind kept me awake so late I was draggy in the morning.

One morning I said, "Mom, sometimes I can't fall asleep."

"Oh, why not?"

"I don't know. I can't get quiet in my mind."

"We all have times like that."

She looked at me a little longer than usual, which made me feel shy. Mom was like an octopus with eight arms that were always full. She swam through her ocean, tending to tasks and people, but rarely did she have time to pause and look very long at one child.

The next night, Mom came by my bed, carrying a small wicker child-sized chair. She put it on the floor and tucked it close to the side of my bed.

"This chair is for your guardian angel. You have your own guardian angel. Just for you. You can speak to her anytime you want, and she will listen. She is here for you with care, understanding, and God's love."

I felt so special having my own guardian angel. Over the years, having that wicker chair was like having an open line to God. When I couldn't sleep, I would look at the chair and know my angel was there. I'd talk to her, and then I could rest better. I don't know whatever happened to that chair, when I lost it, or when God got more distant again. In my life, He has been close at times and far away at times.

I feel a yearning for that closeness right now, open a drawer, and pull out white rosary beads. I finger the rosary while staring at the beads. After some rote prayers that bring me into a more spiritual state, I try talking to God. I notice that the responding voice is not like the voice I heard at the retreat but more like my own voice interpreting my thoughts. Maybe the real voice I heard at the retreat was a one-time gift designed to last my whole life.

Me: Okay, God. Remember that you told me, "and *everything* else you will receive?" Well, I did get a great husband, and I want to thank You for that. My struggle is that we really want a baby, and I am infertile, so what is with that? They want to cut into me and find out why.

God: I did not say you would get everything the way you want.

Me: So, no baby from my body? No cutie that looks like some combo of me and my darling husband? Are You sure? I'm finding it hard to cope with the pain.

God: I feel sorry for your pain, but I never promised that you would give birth in a natural way. How it all unfolds is still up in the air.

Chapter Six

KANGAROO POUCH

Tubal Pregnancy, January 1985

THE NEXT MORNING, the phone rings.

It is Dr. Reinsch. "I guess you really wanted to avoid surgery." His voice sounds chipper.

I sit on the edge of my bed, feeling confused. "What do you mean?"

The doctor continues with a happy tone. "We took your blood sample, and you are pregnant!"

I feel stunned by those magic words and freeze there, unbelieving.

He continues. "You will need a sonogram to rule out an ectopic pregnancy."

I half hear that part because I have sailed up to the sky, so high on joy. He has to repeat twice, "Call the office Monday to schedule the sonogram."

I write down, "Monday, call office for sonogram." I get off the phone, squeal loudly, then laugh and drop to my knees to thank God!

I jump into my car and drive to Steve's office, floating on air. I can't wait to tell him the good news. On the way, I see a CVS. I rush in and skim the shelves until I find the perfect little stuffed animal.

As I pull into the parking lot of the big, rectangular building full of offices, I pass the sign that says, "Marine Science Institute," which is the laboratory where Steve works. I take a breath, and my heart jumps with excitement as I see him walking along the sidewalk. I park, and when he sees me, he walks up to my car.

I smile and must be beaming because Steve asks, "What is it?" He seems to suspect something.

I hop out of the car, and before he can say another word, I whip out a small stuffed kangaroo that has a pouch. I am beyond thrilled as I stare at his green eyes and watch them go from confused to joyous.

"I'm pregnant."

His eyes sparkle for a moment but then flash with fear as he holds the kangaroo. He is wary, wanting to feel the delight but still unsure. He gives me a hug, and I squeeze him tight.

We float into Steve's office and whisper our good news to his friend John, who bounces up from his computer screen and hugs me twice.

———

Over dinner we stare at one another. We are finally going to be parents.

We toast with Martinelli's Apple cider in thin, long-stemmed champagne flutes.

"Here's to us," I say.

"Here's to our family," he says.

We are in a shared dream.

———

In bed that night, as I place my head down on the pillow, I see myself skipping through a green meadow in a long, flowing pastel gown. I feel serene, just the way my mother was during her pregnancies. This matters to me because I have waited so long to be here, to be like her. Before my eyes, a childhood memory unfolds of all of us kids lining up next to Dad on a grassy hill in the side yard of Hazel Hawkins hospital.

He points up with his hand, "Look up there, kids. Mom is in that room."

Excitement mounts after one of us shouts, "Here she comes."

As soon as we see her, we gasp. We all stare as Mom moves the lace curtain and appears with a newborn in her arms. She waves at us with a beatific smile. The green grassy hill is like the freshness of new life that our whole family loved to be part of.

Now as an adult, I want that. I long to be a happy mother, waving from my window, feeling blessed to have a newborn in my arms.

That memory fills my heart, and I whisper, Thank you, God. I love you. I love the world.

I smile softly at a sleeping Steve who climbed into bed after a fourteen-hour workday. As I drift off to sleep, I imagine talking all things baby with my family tomorrow.

———

An hour later, I awake from a pinging sensation in my stomach. Within seconds, it transforms into a sharp pain that sears through my belly.

I try to push the pain away. I lie back in bed with chills that get worse as my whole body shakes. I cannot get warm. From out of nowhere I vomit but that does not relieve the pain.

Fear creeps into my body.

Steve, awakened by my vomiting, mumbles, "You'll be okay. Get some sleep." But when I start to retch uncontrollably, he sits straight up and asks, "Do you want me to call the doctor?"

"I think I can do it," I say, and though it is eleven-thirty at night, I somehow manage to make my way to the phone.

The OB-GYN doesn't mince words. "Get yourself to the ER now. It could be a miscarriage."

My body freezes in terror. The emergency room is over thirty minutes away.

"Think positive, think positive," I whisper to myself as I stand up. Steve gets out of bed and grabs pants and a shirt for me. He delicately helps me dress, noticing that any movement makes my pain worse. I grab a bucket to take with me in the car, just in case.

Once the car begins rolling, I slip into an altered state, where everything irritates me. The music is too cheerful, and the temperature is too cold. Steve, trying to keep his cool, focuses on adjusting the heat.

When we approach the freeway entrance, my stomach lurches, and I vomit into the bucket. Steve quickly pulls over, and I vomit again in the dirt by the side of the road.

The big clock on the wall in the ER reads 12:51 a.m. I double over as a nurse ushers me into an exam room, leaving Steve behind in the waiting room.

The hard exam table is so short that my legs dangle over it. She frowns, jams my feet into the stirrups, and leaves without a word. I shiver from cold and clutch at my sweater to lay it over my hospital gown.

A new sensation, a throbbing in my belly, begins. It turns into a stabbing pain. A wave of panic rushes over me.

The ER doctor, a tall, middle-aged man with a faraway look, examines me at 1:30 a.m. His tired eyes make him look like he is thirty-four hours into a thirty-six-hour shift. A new nurse with soft blond hair enters behind him. She gives me a look of compassion and softness, which I drink in like water in a desert. I look at her nametag. It reads "Anita." I smile, as that is my youngest sister's name.

The doctor presses so hard on my belly that I scoot up the

table in pain. His hands seem rough and lost in unfamiliar territory as he pokes around my pelvic area. He stays wordless. Anita holds my hand and looks at me warmly. Is it okay to look back at her, to use her eyes as an anchor? I blink and glance briefly into her brown eyes, which beam back the only warmth in the cold room. I take that as permission and let myself receive her care. I squeeze my eyes at the next poke from the doctor. Will he ever stop?

Suddenly he steps back and pulls off his gloves. "Well, I have to consult with a gynecologist because I don't know what's wrong with you."

A surge of anger rises as I ask, "Is there anything you can tell me?"

"Well, to be honest, you could just be constipated." Relief washes over me as the heat of anger cools. Could that be it? Could it be that simple?

Before he walks out, he offers, "If you were miscarrying you would be bleeding, and there is no blood; although, it could happen later."

I take a long-needed exhale and think, *Well, it could just be constipation. I could be home and happy within a few hours.*

They take urine; they take blood. After a few hours of poking, prodding, and waiting, I ask for Steve, and my nurse brings him in from the waiting room at three in the morning. He wears a smile on his face, but his scared eyes betray him—he is a wreck.

Steve rushes to my side and grabs my hand. "How are you? What do you know?"

"Nothing. I know nothing."

I am weary, wary, and anxious. Steve tries to distract me with chit-chat as he sits on the uncomfortable-looking rolling stool next to the exam table. We find ourselves almost drifting off to sleep at 4 a.m. when Anita the nurse enters the room. A new doctor, Dr. Morell, who looks just as tired as the first doctor, tells me he is a gynecologist, and that comforts me a bit. At least he is a specialist. Dr. Morell does the same exam, but he is much gentler, and his tone is soothing as he talks me through each step.

Nurse Anita stands near my head. This time I don't hesitate to look at her for support. She smiles, takes my hand, and says, "Squeeze my hand hard when you feel pain."

I squeeze her hand and feel grateful for her presence.

Dr. Morell completes his exam and mumbles something about being back soon with more information. He and Anita leave, and Steve and I sit in silence for a few minutes. But those minutes seem to stretch into forever.

After about an hour, I watch Steve try to rest his head on a Formica counter, but the wheels from under his rolling chair make him slip and slide. I try not to laugh, but it looks so silly, and I am punch-drunk from tiredness.

Steve laughs too and slides on his chair across the room, saying, "Zoom, zoom." But soon, his eyes drop in exhaustion, and he says, "I wish we could go home."

"Me too."

I do want to go home, but as I watch the door, I realize I am holding out for some good news. Compared to a miscarriage, morning sickness or constipation would be great news!

At five in the morning, Dr. Morell comes back into the room. Steve and I sit up, ready for answers. He looks at his clipboard and speaks in a matter-of-fact tone.

"Well, it looks like you could have cystitis, which is a bladder infection, and if that is the case, you will need meds."

We look at one another and sigh in relief. But he isn't done yet.

"Or you could have an ovarian cyst that is part of your pregnancy, and it will diminish."

We nod. We can handle that too.

He isn't done. "Or, this could be the beginning of a miscarriage. When you bleed, that will be the miscarriage. Or you could have a tubal pregnancy."

My mind races around picking up imaginary papers on the floor that have the diagnoses we have been told. No, let it be the easier stuff, like constipation, infection, or morning sickness. The first doctor said it could be a miscarriage, but we are hoping not. I pick up the newest piece of paper that I do not want to believe. Tubal pregnancy. I remember the HSG showed my tubes were clear. The dye went through. So, this can't be. With a quaver in my voice, I ask the doctor to tell us more about it.

Steve and I clench hands as the doctor explains. "Well, the uterus is the only place where the fetus can grow to full term. A tubal is when the fetus lodges and grows in the fallopian tube, which means the pregnancy is not viable."

My eyes grow big and spacy as I picture a fetus stuck in the tube where it wants to grow but has no room. I freeze as that image fills my mind.

"How can we find out if it's a tubal pregnancy?" Steve asks.

"Well, a tubal can only be determined in an operation, a laparoscopy."

"Is that dangerous? Will she be okay?" Steve asks.

The doctor shakes his head. "It's minimally invasive, only a few small incisions, low risk." His voice takes a lower, slower, more deliberate tone. "Not that it happens often, but if the pregnancy continues to grow, then the fallopian tube could rupture and kill you."

I was suddenly wide awake. "Wait, what? It could kill me?" My head swims in waters too deep. "I don't understand. What causes a tubal pregnancy?"

"One possibility is that the Dalkon Shield you used in the past for birth control could have scarred your fallopian tubes."

"How?"

"The Dalkon Shield has a history of causing pelvic inflammatory disease, which can result in scarring." I am sinking further under water, when this memory appears in my head: I clutched my gut and felt an internal burning in my pelvis a few weeks after having the Dalkon Shield inserted in my twenties. That pain subsided only after I had the Shield removed.

The doctor seems to notice my alarm and says, "But please keep in mind that this could still be something very minor like a bladder infection. We just don't know right now. I will need you to return tonight at 6 p.m. for a blood test."

After the doctor leaves the room, I dress slowly, feeling the weight of things that could go wrong.

With sleepy heads and gloomy spirits, Steve and I walk ourselves out of the hospital at six in the morning and climb into our car. A dark cloud seems to trail us even though a shy dawn breaks as we arrive at our house.

As I get out of the car, I squint. The pale sun may be a sign of hope that everything will be okay.

———

Steve sleeps a little, then goes into work for the rest of the day. When he comes home, I look at his tired face and realize he is in no condition to drive me back to the hospital for the 6 p.m. blood test. I call my friend Anne, who comes right over.

"You ready?" Anne says and jangles her car keys. I go upstairs, put on some jeans, and halfway back down the stairs, I am hit with acute pain in my belly. I yelp. I can't move. Steve, concerned, runs to help me down the rest of the steps. Anne holds my side and opens the door, and as we leave, Steve gives me a few towels to take with me in case I vomit. Oh, God, not again. Please, Lord.

I watch Steve turn and go back in the house. As he closes the front door, I miss him and wish he was going with me. As Anne drives through town, my gut hurts, and a lurching sensation begins. Anne pulls over, and I vomit in the gutter. It hurts more than it did yesterday, and my heart beats faster from a rising sense of danger. When we turn into the driveway at Kaiser, I see the sign for the lab where I was supposed to get the bloodwork but I know that I am not going there.

I turn to Anne. "Take me straight to the emergency room."

She does. After she parks, she hops out of the car and runs to the entrance, commanding, "I need a wheelchair now."

My legs dangle out of the open passenger door, and she eases me into the chair.

As Anne rolls me through the double doors, she says to the staff, "Hey, she might vomit."

An attendant places a green plastic bucket in my lap and takes the reins from Anne.

I constantly throw up as I am rushed through the ER waiting room. From the green blur of the room, I see a few waiting patients put their hands to their faces and look disgusted at my noisy retching.

Time slows as we enter the exam room. It looks exactly like the room I waited in for hours earlier that morning. Afraid they might do that to me again, I summon my energy and say, "I need that beta blood test right away."

I try to take care of myself, but my body has a mind of its own, and I swallow back the terror, so I can make it through these dark woods. I try to listen, but information comes to me in pieces, as if chunks of disconnected things are happening.

A middle-aged, dark-haired surgeon enters the room and introduces himself. "I am Dr. O'Patry, and we are going to do a pelvic exam and take your blood."

I cross my fingers as they draw blood, in hopes that the blood test will prove I have a uterine pregnancy.

Later, Dr. O'Patry announces, "We will do a sonogram next, and you need fluid in your abdomen so we can get a clear view."

A catheter is inserted, an invasion so complete I can barely stand it. When they fill my bladder with liquid, I squeeze my own hand and count while looking at the ceiling to distract myself. I watch intently as the nurse puts gel on a wand and places it over my water-filled belly. She moves the wand around as she and the doctor stare at images on a screen that I can't see. I look at their faces for a sign, but they are trained to have the dead eyes that tell you nothing.

Then, I hear the dreaded words from Dr. O'Patry: "There is no gestational sac in your uterus."

I gasp, and the back of my head swarms with the buzzing of a hundred panicked little bees with nowhere to go.

The doctor's words reverberate in my ears, and I pull as far into myself as I can go. I see myself tumbling down a cliff and hitting sharp rocks as I fall forever.

The doctor is still looking at the screen and talking. "I see a mass in the tube and am pretty sure it's a tubal pregnancy like I'd feared." He gets right in my face and, with urgency, says, "You need surgery tonight—and depending on what I find, either a laparotomy or a laparoscopy, probably a laparotomy."

A wave of terror and mistrust washes over me. Who is this guy? What is he saying? Surgeons just want to cut you to solve problems. Like a mechanic. Like my body is a machine to him. He doesn't care about me as a person. I summon all my will, look him in the eye, which is too close to my face, and say, "You're scaring me."

His demeanor changes as he registers my distress. He walks slowly to the foot of my bed to give me more space. His tone of voice becomes compassionate. "I know this is not what you wanted and you're scared. But the fetus is growing in your fallopian tube. Remember, when it ruptures, which might happen soon, it could kill you."

Kill me? Oh, that's right. I get it now. I nod yes to the surgery.

The doctor exits, and Anne is allowed to return to my room. She rushes to my side.

I tell her, "I'm overwhelmed. It's over. The pregnancy is not viable."

She squeezes my hand in both of hers. "I am so sorry."

I feel my heart break. I realize I need to call Steve, who I am sure must be wringing his hands, anxiously waiting for news.

When he answers the phone, I tell him the bad news.

He mumbles, "Oh, I don't want to come to Kaiser." His voice sounds groggy and faraway. "Anne can handle it."

Anne can handle it? I get off the phone and frown. Maybe he just woke up, and his usual caring self is still asleep. I try to give him grace, but a little black cloud forms behind my eyes. Is he really not coming?

After six solid hours of constant pain, I start numbering pain levels so I can track them. Why? I don't know. I can't control any of it. My body has betrayed me. But the numbering brings me into the present moment, so I don't totally disappear in some other reality that might show up. Nope, nope, this is my body. This is my life right now. Ouch. On a scale of one to ten that was a six, now a seven. Now a nine. Oh, a few breaths with no pain. Enjoy this. Oh, here comes a four.

But the constancy of pain keeps me taut as a string that begins to tear. I might unravel and break.

Steve appears at the door to my room. Anne smiles, squeezes my hand, and knows it is time for her to go home. I watch as she leaves, grateful she was here. I feel unsure about Steve.

He hugs me, and I melt into him sobbing. "You didn't want to come."

He touches my face and says, "I was sleepy when you called and didn't quite get what was happening. Of course I want to be here."

I sigh in relief for one less problem.

———

They prep me for surgery by injecting me with Demerol, which weaves wooziness through me like lightning as the nurse says, "We call this the golden wave."

All the stabbing pelvic pain I endured for six hours disappears on a dime. I cannot believe this is possible. It is like a magic spell from a fairy godmother. And I am grateful.

They wheel me to surgery, and I smile in anticipation. When we get to the operating room, I am fascinated by the white lights, and I say, "This looks just like on television." I chat with Kathy, the nurse anesthetist, and get a glimpse of Dr. O'Patry as he comes toward me . . . and that is all I remember.

I am dopey, and my bed shakes as they wheel me to the recovery room. I shudder with cold and half open my eyes to see Steve in the doorway craning his neck to peek in. I think they wheel me to another room. All I want is sleep and more blankets to fend off the chill that sweeps through my whole body.

Chapter Seven

POST-SURGERY

Maternity Ward

IT IS DARK, so it must be night. I try to turn to my side as I sleep, but my lower body does not budge. It is completely numb. Maybe this is temporary. I try again. Dead. Alarm rises in my body. I am confused and return to a muddled sleep.

I hear sounds of babies being born all hours of the night. Am I dreaming? My head is full of drugs to recover from surgery, so I don't know what is real.

In the morning, I awake to hear more clearly the cries of the newborns and the cheers of celebrating families as they walk past my room.

Am I in a maternity ward? I just lost a baby. There is no way they would put me here, right? Oh, my God. My lower body is still numb. My mind is numb from the sheer meanness of putting baby-loss patients in the same ward with baby-gain patients. I pull a pillow over my ears to drown the intrusive sounds of the brass-ring-winning parents and their new babies.

———

As nurses clear out of his way, Dr. O'Patry comes in, holding a clipboard and looking somber. "I did have to perform the laparotomy on you."

I nod and listen intently to this person who has put his hands inside my body and made life-altering decisions.

He continues. "I had to remove the fetus and four inches of the tube."

I know he had to, but hearing it is still a shock. When I hear the word "fetus" my mind goes down a blind tunnel. I'm thinking, *You removed the fetus? What did you do with it? Where does it go?* I have to know and don't dare want to know.

I stop myself from continuing down the tunnel, because I know it might make me crazy, and that can't end anywhere good. Just further into the dark recesses of my wounded soul. I shake my head to rattle away the darkness.

The doctor says, "I wasn't able to really examine the tube, as there was so much blood." He looks at his open hand for a second, pauses, then clears his throat. "The other tube might be okay; I found some 'milky adhesions,' which are due to the Dalkon Shield, probably."

This is too much information for me to handle at once. He is the surgeon. He is back to business, already onto the next possible solution—my other fallopian tube. The good news does give me a dollop of hope.

When the doctor exits, and the door is open, I see a grinning father walk by with a blue "It's a boy" mylar balloon. I sense a desire to fold into myself, but right then Steve enters my hospital room with a bouquet of pastel flowers. He tells me the surgery lasted from midnight until three in the morning.

Steve takes my hand and strokes my hair. "I'm just glad you're okay." He looks at me with his compassionate blue-gray eyes, pools of love that make me feel more solid. His eyes show a touch of fear as he tells me, "Last night, I couldn't find where you were in the hospital. I kept asking and getting nowhere, so I started introducing myself as 'Dr. Schroeter,' and soon all these doors opened until I found you."

I giggle at the thought that this guy who usually follows all the rules was assertive enough to pretend his PhD in ecology was an MD.

After Steve leaves, I look at the big clock on my hospital room wall. Nothing happens to shift its shape, its numbers, its big and small hands. It ticks and tocks the time away, like nothing changes. In the space of twelve hours, my whole life has changed. My pregnancy is over, my baby is gone, my body doesn't work right.

Later, when I need to use the restroom, I find that I can't sit up. I try not to panic. I call for a nurse. She brings a bedpan. My eyes are watery with shock.

After the nurse leaves, my roommate Jean, who has been here three days longer than me, watches me. She sees how disoriented I look and says, "You just got out of surgery. That is why you can't move well."

"How long does that last?"

"You will get better daily, but due to pain, they will give you the heavy meds these first few days. Your body can get addicted to it, so after about three days, they cut you down to lesser strength drugs."

"Thanks. They told me none of this." It helps soften the hard knock of shock when I know things, and I am surprised and bothered that the medical team does not tell me what to expect.

I drift off to sleep for the night to the sound of beeping monitors. I get jostled awake at midnight by nurses with needles who grab my hand, adjust cords, and tap the bags of fluid.

One says, "You have a fever, so we have to monitor for possible pneumonia and infection."

I like that they monitor me, but I also long for a good night's sleep. How can the body heal when it's being awakened all the time? I am grumpy from all this body invasion and poor sleep.

By the next day my fever has subsided, and my head is less foggy. My fertility specialist, Dr. Reinsch, comes in just as I try to get up for the first time by myself. His face is kind as he sits down next to me and says, "I'm sad. I just found out today about your tubal pregnancy."

I like that he can sit in this heavy truth with me, and I linger in this moment of connection. His caring presence seems to soak up some of the weight of all my sorrow and hurt.

"Let's talk about your options," he says after a while.

I nod although I am not sure I am ready to think about the future.

"You can try in a few months to get pregnant again and risk another ectopic or do a laparoscopy to check the fertility of the other tube."

I tremble when he says "another ectopic" but I also need to hang onto this tiny seed of hope that the other tube may be viable.

The soft cries of newborns on the ward push and pull at my heart. I wonder where they are. There must be a nursery nearby. I want to go see the babies, but ominous music in my head warns me of danger. This is my first walk on my own, and I follow my ears toward the baby sounds. I make a turn and see a large glass wall. Behind the wall are rows of little wrinkled beings wrapped in swaddling clothes. I am taken aback and mesmerized at the same time. I stare as they yawn and stretch their fingers and faces in all kinds of ways. They are so tiny yet so real. So real. Then my head fills with the sound of a loud, angry train coming right at me as I stand on the tracks. I can't take it. My legs shake. I am going to fall apart. I press my hands into the cool, clean glass and try to take a deep breath.

A blond, middle-aged woman appears next to me. She asks, "Which one is yours?" Her words are a knife that slices me open. My knees buckle, and she grabs my arm to keep me from falling. I look at her and am so gutted, so stripped of any armor, that I stutter, "None of them. I just lost a baby."

"I am so very, very sorry."

I want to cry, but I can't stand up much longer on these wobbly legs.

She asks, "Is there anything I can do for you?"

"Yes, can you help me walk back to my room?"

She holds my arm as we walk, and I tell her about my ectopic pregnancy.

When we get to my room she offers, "May God bless you."

That feels so good to hear. Dumb idea going to see the babies. I wasn't ready, but here is some love back, and I let that blessing spill over me for comfort.

———

The next day, Dr. Reinsch enters my room at 6 a.m. As he looks at my chart, he says, "Maybe you'll go home tomorrow."

I feel both afraid to go home to some unknown future and afraid to stay here, where knife wounds from insensitive remarks and poking and prodding claim my days. A heaviness presses on my chest, and I tear up.

A nurse enters and looks at my teary eyes. She says, "Your crying is not only psychological but physical."

"What do you mean?"

"The hormonal change of pregnancy can cause weeping. You have postpartum depression."

"How can that be? I didn't have a baby."

"You still had a major hormonal change."

Another stab with a knife. Postpartum depression with no baby?

After she leaves, I pick up my journal, the one I had Steve bring me from home. The one I had by my bed. I always have a spiral-bound, blank-paged journal by my bedside to draw and write in. I've kept personal diaries off and on since I was fifteen. I sometimes write down dreams in the morning. At night I write about my day. Sometimes, I pick up a pencil or pen and am compelled to draw, like it is the only thing that will bring some sanity to whatever threatens to overwhelm me. No thinking, just drawing and writing.

I fill an entire page with a drawing of my fallopian tubes, one amputated with a ragged gouge. I grab a red colored pencil and color the gouge and let bloody drops of red blood fill the bottom of the page.

In the middle of the day, my surgeon, Dr. O'Patry, comes by and removes my staples. I feel freer without those metal clips on my belly. He confirms what Dr. Reinsch said, that I will be able go home tomorrow.

I touch the area of my body above the bikini line and feel nothing. "Why does it feel numb over the incision?"

"I had to cut your nerves, and they won't heal." Cut nerves? They won't heal? A shiver runs through me. I take in the full view of my belly, which looks puffed up. I look three months pregnant, which seems cruel.

The doctor notices my staring and says, "The distension in your belly is mostly gas." He grabs his papers and leaves me.

All alone, I close my eyes, and my mind walks down a dark road. I imagine Doctor O'Patry walking into my room, carrying the gestational sac in a paper bag. He says, "You can take it home and let it grow, and in nine months, it will be a baby." He sets the paper bag down on the bed, laughs at me, and walks away.

I open my eyes, shake my head, and force that image to fade. I perk up my ears when I overhear a doctor congratulate a new mother down the hall. My imagination takes flight again. I create the following scenario: The woman who just gave birth is huddled with the doctor. They are whispering. She tells the doctor that she doesn't want to keep the baby. Knowing my situation, they nod to each other, and the doctor brings me her baby to take home. I feel this pressure in my head insisting, "This could happen. I need this to happen."

I get this way—adamant about something needing to

happen, and soon. My ram-like head with big horns barreling through, big horns that might knock others out of my way to thrust forward and get what I want. I sigh and lie back in the bed. It is either thrust forward or this: The loud sound of the train barreling toward me, then jamming into me as I stand frozen on the tracks, driving right through my body without a care, breaking me, leaving a gaping bloody hole in my center as a baby wails until the sound trails away. A baby cut out of me disappears—but to where? Somewhere I can't follow. Where do I go next? As if by a siren call, I am drawn to new babies crying behind a glass divider, a glass so thick, I can't get in, babies so close, yet unreachable.

The phone ringing jars me back to the present. I answer, "Hello?"

"It's Mom. How are you?" Her voice invites me to come in from wandering down tortured, bumpy roads in the far wastelands of dark, impossible lands.

I say, "I'm okay. I might go home soon. Mostly sad."

"Oh, I'm so sorry. I was thinking about you at Mass today and said a prayer for you."

"You prayed for *me*?"

"I am flying in to take care of you when you get home. I will call later with the details."

"Oh, thank you so much, Mom." I get off the phone and smile in gratitude. I close my eyes and see her as a small light coming toward me in the dark wasteland.

A few hours later, the phone rings again, and I hear my mother's voice. I expect her to say, "I will be on the next plane."

Instead, she says, "I can't come until later in the week."

It doesn't occur to me to ask her why not because a familiar fogginess fills my brain, and I fold into myself. I shrug. "Okay, Mom. Bye." I hang up the phone, hurt, even though I know this is just a delay.

Chapter Eight

BRAIDS

Mom and Me

I AM as thin as a threadbare blanket, porous and floating alone in space. I need something to hold on to. I grab a pillow and press my forehead into it. I gulp back tears, tighten my spine, and breathe.

I am taken back to my childhood, with so many of us kids bouncing around but each one hungry for a few extra private minutes with Mom or Dad. It was always like this growing up with eleven brothers and sisters. I would enter the house after walking home from school alone and want to tell Mom that I won the spelling bee and earned a plastic statue of the Blessed Virgin Mary; that I'm angry because Sister Teresa hit my bare legs with a stick; that a blond girl laughed, saying that, since there were so many of us Warren kids, each one of us must be "mediocre."

I don't say any of these things. Mom is busy tending to kids who are yelling louder than me. And so I sink away and disappear into my own fantasy world.

As I look out the window from my hospital bed, I think of my mother's life. She came of age during the Great Depression of the 1930s and waited for my father to come home from war after World War II.

After her wedding ceremony in 1945, the priest asked her, "Ramona, how many children are you going to have?"

With a beaming smile she answered, "Oh, about a dozen."

Both my parents wanted a big family, and she ended up birthing twelve children. Easily, from what I knew. I was the fourth child.

She would smile and say, "I have four under four" while folding mountains of cloth diapers. Forever working to keep the huge household running, she always wore an apron and was usually faced away from me. Her hands forever busy. At the ironing board. At the stove. At the sink. At the washing machine.

When Steve and I leave the hospital the next day, I am forced to go home empty-handed. No baby to hold, no mother to hold my hand. My body has been violated, and my heart has been broken. I feel like a failure.

We travel the long forty-five minutes from the hospital to our home in silence. I close my eyes. I don't want to know what is going on outside this car window. Once home, I pull myself out of the passenger side door in the carport of our humble beige condo. As I walk around the corner to enter the house, I burst out crying. When I left this house, I was pregnant, now I am not and may never be. I take to my bed and let it swallow me.

Jon, our neighbor and Steve's best friend, comes over later with pizza and salad, so I drag myself to the dining room. I push my salad around with a fork, feeling disoriented and withdrawn.

Jon looks at me with sympathetic eyes and says, "You've had a brush with death—and come out of it very well."

I blink, look at Jon, nod, and go back to my pizza and my inner thoughts. I hadn't seen it that way, and it makes me feel better about being so fragile.

A few days later, Steve picks up my mother at the airport, and I hear their voices as she arrives. My heart pounds with longing, then switches to fear, as I tell myself Mom will be of little comfort. She won't understand this pain at all.

Soon, I hear my mother's footsteps coming down the hall. I rub the soft edge of the blanket between my fingers. As she appears in the doorway, I have two strong urges—one is to hide; the other is to be held. My head is spacey, but my body feels tight. I can't move.

Mom enters my bedroom. I can't tell her I am disappointed that she arrived days late.

Short, solid, and a little speedy, with a small, sturdy, old family suitcase with weathered leather straps, she walks toward my bed. I look at her for only a second, glancing briefly at her with coldness covering my hurt. She stares at me with compassion, which stings because I cannot take it in.

Eager to be helpful, she unlocks her suitcase and reaches into it. "I brought you the doll you had as a child." She pulls out a glamorous woman doll, in a strapless black velvet dress. I look her over. I am mute. Why is she here? Is this doll on her way to some party? The 1950s plastic twelve-inch toy has a vapid red lipstick smile and flirty eyes. It is like this doll is in a different reality in her carefree twenties, a single, babyless, happy world. She was fun when I was a kid at home, imagining growing up to date and dance. But now? It is like she's in costume and has walked onto the wrong set. I frown and look away.

Mom realizes the doll is not working and puts it aside. She does not give up. Next, she pulls out a brush and comb.

"Would you like me to braid your hair like I did when you were little?"

I am taken aback, surprised she is returning to our childhood routines. I soften for a moment as I realize she took time to think about me as a child and what might feel homey, familiar, or comforting. This warms my heart, but I am oversensitive, and that blip of sweetness turns to a sour taste in my mouth.

"No," I say. My mind goes down an old road, recalling the morning in third grade when Mom was rushing to braid my long hair just as Dad yelled that we were running late for school. My mother grabbed the scissors and cut four inches off my braids—without even asking. I was the only sister with braids, and those long braids made me feel unique in a sea of look-alikes. Every school morning Mom would spend five minutes just braiding my hair and applying ribbons over the rubber bands. It had been our special time.

After she cut them, I shivered a little and frowned as she finished braiding the few inches that were left. She never apologized, and I never complained. No time. Had to keep up with the pack, even if it made me invisible.

Now, I'm all grown up. I don't need my party-girl doll. I don't want little-girl braids. She is trying to reach me. I look into her eyes with longing. My neck feels tight. I am stuck. She gets it too—that these efforts are not helpful.

She slowly closes her suitcase, moves to the back of my bed, and looks at me with searching eyes.

"What can I do for you?"

I shrug, feeling more like a child than a grown-up. "I don't know."

She looks into my eyes and says, "I am so sorry."

I look up into her eyes. "I … I lost my baby."

Her face pulses with compassion as she says, "What a terrible loss. I feel so sad for you."

As her words sink in, my body relaxes some to feel seen by her.

She had moments like this when we were little, where she paused and paid attention to our needs. But they were rare, and we all understood why. She worked thirty-six-hour shifts as a mother and housewife, and any extra demand beyond feed, clothe, and bathe would often be met (if at all) by someone running on fumes.

I never saw her weak. She rarely sat down. If she suffered, she never showed it. When I was a kid, I just saw her as a strong, solid force of steady caretaking. Invincible. She would whistle cheerfully through her pregnancies, give birth, then take efficient care of easily born babies.

Mom looks at me firmly. I hear a sorrow in her voice I have never heard before. "You know, I had two miscarriages. One after Kenny was born and one after Maria was born."

I am shocked by this information. My eyes grow as big as saucers. She continues, her voice heavy with grief. I am riveted to the spot because she has never been this vulnerable with me before.

"Their loss hit me hard. I think of those two as souls sitting next to Jesus in heaven. I pray to them every day."

I stare at a woman I have never met. Who is she? I have only known the strong, invincible Mom.

She lost two babies? They stay in her heart? She thinks of them every day?

I am stunned. My head explodes, and the hard-set pixels of "This is my mother" scramble to rearrange themselves into something new. They turn into a meadow with sweet yellow flowers. I look at my mother and drink in the softened contours of her face. She is meeting me in the meadow, in a field of grief.

"Mom, I never knew that you lost two babies. I am blown away and heartbroken for you."

My insides loosen all the knots that, up to this point, I thought were needed to keep me together. To keep me from falling apart. I look at my mother anew and linger. I see her through my eyes that are pure "full-joy" and gratitude.

It is like she saw me coming, turned to face me, and made room on her lap where I could climb up and lay my weary head against her warm bosom. For as long as I needed. Mother to daughter. Mother to mother. Mothers who lose babies. Mothers who mourn lost babies.

A yellow light from above fills the room, passes between us, and fills my spirit in some permanent new way.

I am all smiles as Mom hands me gifts from her sisters. Auntie Anne gives me a case with toiletries and a little ceramic cow that says, "Hang in there." I chuckle.

Auntie Marian sends me a cozy pink nightgown. I cry reading her letter. "I'm sorry you lost the baby," she writes. "I know how much you want one, and someday, you will have one."

———

On Wednesday, Mom leads me on a long walk, longer than usual. She encourages me to keep going, but I get tired, so we sit on a bench, looking up at the eucalyptus trees in the park. Mom talks about family history and gets teary talking about her father, who we called "Nano." "Nano helped plant those giant euca-lyptus trees in the grove off the road as we drive to Monterey. He is always present for me—when I walk among your eucalyptus trees, I feel him here." I am so loving this new part of Mom, where she shares about communicating with her beloved ones who have passed on.

Mom's eyes soften as she stares at the trees, and she has a serene smile as we walk back into the house. She looks into my kitchen and asks, "What do you want me to make for dinner?"

I ask for a childhood favorite, "olla," that she and her Spanish mother used to make.

She places a big chunk of meat and some *fideos y garbanzos* (noodles and beans) in a pot and slowly cooks them together in broth on top of the stove. Once cooked, she divides all three parts separately onto our plates.

The hearty smell of fall-off-the-bone meat enters my nostrils and takes me to our childhood home, where every night around the kitchen table we gathered and ate together. Even if I felt lonely during the day, eating warm food together every night nurtured my body and soul.

I taste the tender meat. I twirl my fork around soft noodles and scoop up a few tasty beans. Olla warms my insides, just like it did when I was a child.

Mom stays a week, cooking, cleaning, and comforting. As Steve loads Mom's worn brown suitcase into our car, my heart bursts with love and gratitude.

We hug goodbye before she climbs into the car. I hold her tight, savoring this rare, precious, one-on-one time with my mother. She has filled me with so much, with not only the warm childhood food that sated some loneliness but also the gift of a new part of her, her familiarity and openness in loss.

As the car pulls away, I shed a tear, a tear I am happy to feel and not afraid to show. I have learned from her to be more open about my grief and my loss. I can own, linger in, honor, and ride the waves of my sorrow up and down without denial.

———

Steve is sweet and attentive as we drive to church a few days later on a Sunday morning. He puts his warm hand on mine as we sit off to the side. In the middle of the service, I get in a line to receive Holy Communion. The comforting ritual allows me to drop into an open place in my soul, where I am allowing my grief without hiding. As I walk down the center aisle, it is just me and God. I take a breath and am surprised to hear myself say to God, "Help me. I'm drowning." I feel humbled.

When I get to the altar, the priest makes the sign of the cross while holding the next wafer, looks at me, and says, "The Body of Christ."

I answer, "Amen" as he places it in my hand. I turn to walk back down the aisle, put the wafer in my mouth, and let it melt on my tongue. A warmth rushes through my body. Once back in my pew, I cradle my pain, bow my head and ask, "God, why? Why me?"

It is time to sit still and be fully in this experience. Like opening a closed book, I try to make space in my mind for some answer in the universe about why I need this trial, this terrible ordeal, this brush with death and baby loss. I need more than just shrugging my shoulders and accepting random fate. Questions float up. Am I supposed to become a deeper person? Am I experiencing this so that I can help people in similar situations? What am I supposed to learn?

Chapter Nine

DIFFERENT PLANETS: WORK UNDER THE SPELL OF GRIEF

1985

I SIFT through unfamiliar papers and tap my rusty brain with my finger to get it to kick into gear.

Two weeks out of the hospital, I feel lethargic and have been napping during the day, but I am scheduled to give a lecture in the bioenergetic training program. I am anxious the night before, fighting sleep to stay up late to prepare. I pull out lecture material and stare at the papers in front of me. They look foreign. Part of the "before" world. How can I squirt some oil on these rusty brain gears? I have been residing in a cave of pain and loss, and all my focus has been on the emotional world of coming up from trauma.

As the words on the page become clearer, I nod, and my cognitive brain starts its engine. I notice a shift toward feeling lighter because I am doing something that distracts me from the burden of my grief. The light sparks a seed of excitement as I dig in and realize I know this material. I'm not just a broken body and grieving soul. I have a brain that knows something outside of my trauma drama. I focus on how to make my seminar as engaging as possible for the students. I like how this activity keeps my fragility at bay.

Because my stomach muscles were cut in surgery, I am not strong enough to drive, so the next day, Steve drives me downtown. He sits in the waiting room while I enter the classroom and shyly smile at the students who look up at me.

For this training, the students are sitting on the floor so they can go from the cognitive lessons to some experiential body work in order to practice somatic tools.

I pull my sweater closer, wishing I had on one more layer of clothing to shield my vulnerability. I know I cannot sit on the floor in my condition, so I ask a student to bring me a chair.

As I gather my notes, I take a slow breath to muster a professional demeanor. Once I have their attention, I get lost in the topic of the dynamics of the therapeutic process when working with psychopathic personalities. Strength comes through my voice as I am able to make the complex concepts understandable. I look up often during my lecture. Students nod and ask thoughtful questions. My body becomes more solid from the inside out, and my spirit lifts. By the end of the session, I feel a surge of energy I haven't felt in months.

As I gather my papers, I hear clapping. I look up in surprise. Either they valued the seminar or they felt sorry for me because I showed up still a wounded bird. Probably both.

Steve stands as I leave the classroom and asks, "How did it go?"

"Great." He gives me a big smile, and my chest blossoms with both pride and calm.

But the calm doesn't last.

That night a dark cloud follows me to bed and I cannot sleep. I write to God in my journal as my trauma reawakens and pushes its ugly head up from underground.

My body feels broken. I have been cut open, and I almost bled to death. They sliced me open from hip to hip. The doctor wrote that he had never seen so much blood in his life. My baby had no place to grow. She was trying to make it to the uterus but got stuck on the road in the fallopian tube and tried to grow there. And she did, but there is not enough room there.

As I write it, I say this next part aloud, repeating it in order to help me accept it all: "Why couldn't they grab the fetus and put her into the right place? She outgrew her nest, she ruptured my tube and died, and now, I feel drawn toward death myself."

Then, I am silent again as I write. *I do okay, then I plunge down this well again. I am trying to accept it all and it's hard. Dear Lord, do you give a shit?*

———

For the next few weeks, everything leads to a nap. Teach a short gig. Nap. Brush my teeth. Nap. Eat dinner. Nap.

After one particularly long nap, Steve sits at my bedside with concern in his eyes. His voice is crisp and clear. "When do you think you can return to a regular work schedule?"

I feel pressure from him that I want to push away. I try to focus. "When I'm ready. Not now."

Steve continues. "You know we need both our incomes to pay the bills."

He's right, but I just want him to disappear so I can go back to sleep. I want to say, "Leave me alone. I resent having to work when I'm clearly not ready."

I emphasize the differences between us: *You're the man; you should support us! Yeah, maybe that's sexist of me, but you had a father who was a doctor! You had money growing up. Your teenage jobs were all voluntary. I worked in my Dad's grocery store from the time I was ten! I've been working my whole damn life!* I say none of it.

Instead, I swallow all my anger and say, "I know we do." I slowly get up from the bed and reach for a clean shirt. I shrug. "I can go back to work next week."

———

One week later, I am back at work, and the place is foreign to me.

A client walks in wearing a serene, happy smile. She plops down, leans forward, and eagerly begins talking too fast. "Well, after I get all my papers in, I am pretty sure I will be accepted into the doctoral program. It's a three-year-long post-master's."

I reach inside me to summon a voice that might sound encouraging. "Oh, you're feeling hopeful and sound excited."

She continues with enthusiasm. "Yes, and then I will get a teaching post because I already know some of the teachers from my undergraduate work, and they like me."

I can't relate. Her chipper attitude about future joy makes me cringe inside. I think, *Who cares? What future? How can you get excited about anything? Why do people bother making plans?*

We are on different planets. I feel so distant from her and know I should be going toward her, but I can't. I am floating further out to sea on a thinning chunk of melting ice in a slow-moving fjord. I do my best to show some interest, because I know she deserves that. I say, "I admire your confidence, as I know you want to be a professor."

But then my mind drifts out to sea again. Out to sea where dreams don't come true.

I look at her and think, *Why are you in the future? There is nothing there. The promises are unreal. It is stupid to feel any joy.* My jaw tightens. I am slipping further away, barely tethered to this world, this time, this place.

My client's voice brings me back. "Then after teaching for ten years, I will get a bigger salary and plan to travel to Europe often."

I repeat, with no enthusiasm, "You love to travel and see the world. Good for you."

She looks at me as if confused. Then she frowns.

Why is she frowning? Did I miss something she said?

"All you do is reflect what I say. That isn't helping me." She focuses her intense gaze on my face, demanding a response.

I'm suddenly anxious and squirmy but try to keep my composure. "What? Tell me more about what you mean." I look at her warmly and wait patiently, hoping my presence is now inviting.

After a moment she says, "I feel lonely and want to explore that more."

She felt lonely while I was off on the ice floe. That makes sense. I get that her future dreams are also a distraction from what makes her more vulnerable—her isolation and loneliness.

I bring it back to us and say, "We can do that. Let's start with our relationship. Tell me how you are experiencing me right now."

The rest of the session goes well. As I drive home that night, I realize that her confrontation was a gift. She dropped into a more vulnerable place by admitting her loneliness, which helped snap me back to shore, back from the icy distance of my own pain. Being more present with her kept my pain at bay.

Feeling good is a sweater I haven't worn in a while, and I'm not sure it fits. But as I pull into the driveway, I still feel good, as if some warm layers of belonging are returning to my body.

Those layers weave together into a thicker layer as I try to heal, but I am still concerned about my body's integrity. I know the next chapter is supposed to include a laparoscopy and efforts to get pregnant again. I hope the other fallopian tube is unscarred and unscathed and that a smooth ride will allow the fetus to slide all the way to the uterus, the only true nest for it to grow.

But what if something goes wrong again? I want to avoid trouble and have a baby easily.

Maybe I should skip the hospital world and go straight to adoption.

———

The next morning, I watch butter slowly melt onto my toast. Steve gives me a kiss on the cheek. "Did you get any sleep last night?"

I nod. "A little bit. I'm thinking about the option of adoption."

He pulls his head back in surprise and says, "Oh. I want to try again before we try to adopt."

My body tenses, and I feel a heaviness in my chest. I exhale. I want to say something positive, but all I can manage is, "Umm hmmm, okay." I slice into a red apple, and my anxiety rises as I recall the needles, speculums, injections, and body invasions. My hand holding the knife squirms and the next cut is jagged.

I hear Steve say, "I don't want my kid wearing a silly hat like that."

I look up and realize he is flipping through a magazine and referring to a glossy color photo of a child in some advertisement. He shows me the photo, and I smile at how cute the innocent little three-year-old looks. Steve has a thing about hats; he thinks many look stupid. Steve's face lingers on the photo, and his eyes seem to soften. He looks like a man who is eager to be a dad. I gaze at him with sympathy. He pulls me close and holds me.

My anxiety fades away, and I ask, "Do you want me to have the laparoscopy to check if my other tube is open?"

He nods. "Yes, I do." He does not include his usual qualifier, "But it is your decision."

I lean into his warm chest and breathe in rhythm with him. Maybe I can give it one more try. The important thing is to become a parent, however it happens. I sigh and think about the cuteness of all the three-year-old toddlers in the world. Toddlers whom others get to parent and watch grow. Other people get to be parents but probably not us. When he lets me go, I tighten back up into my usual impatience, go to the table, pick up my journal, and write:

GRIEF is when
carefree
happiness
can be shattered
by the smile
of a small child
who belongs,
who always
belongs —
to somebody else.

Chapter Ten

FERTILIZABLE: TRYING AGAIN

WE ARE BACK at the fertility clinic. The laparoscopic surgery to check my remaining fallopian tube only lasts twenty minutes, and I am awake an hour later.

Dr. Reinsch says, "Your tube is clear, not blocked. The dye went right through." He sounds almost optimistic.

I am hit by a jolt of excitement.

"I had to cut a few adhesions, and the distal end looks a little odd, but you are fertilizable." He adds, "I can see an egg descending, and I recommend you go home and try to get pregnant."

My eyes widen with this window of new possibility.

———

The next few months are a blur of not getting my period, hoping to be pregnant, taking a pregnancy test, and seeing it come out negative. I have ridden this roller coaster before, but it's still frustrating.

I hold another negative pregnancy test in my hand after the hopeful urinating on a stick. I look at it with a sigh of annoyance. The phone rings.

My sister Maria's voice is filled with joy. "Hey, guess what? Cefe had her baby girl."

I gasp and freeze. I want to respond happily about the birth of my first niece, but no words will form. Even worse, tears start to fall.

Maria gently asks, "Are you okay?"

I do not want to ruin the mood of her joy, so I contain my crying and ask, "Did Mom give Cefe the wicker chair?"

"Yes. How did you know about that?"

"Mom promised it to her first granddaughter."

———

A month later my period is three days late. I sit on the toilet and urinate on the stick. I hold it and wait as time ticks by too slowly. I turn and shake the stick. Can this be? It's the right color: I am pregnant! I gasp in disbelief and fold my hands in prayer. "Thank you, Lord."

I go into my bedroom and get down on my knees. "Please Lord," I beg and start to stand up but then pause, kneel back down, and add, "But your will, not mine, be done."

I grab the phone and schedule a blood test at Kaiser the next day, hoping it confirms the home test. I hope the sonogram will show a uterine pregnancy and that I don't end up in the emergency room vomiting in six hours of severe pain like the last time. I push away that bad memory so it won't drown my happy mood.

I get back on my knees because I have more to say to God. I repeat, "Your will, not mine, be done." I implore with excitement, "But I hope I get beautifully fatter for the next nine months, buy my first ever maternity clothes, and a have a healthy baby around March. This is my wish list. Thanks for listening. In the name of the Father, the Son, and the Holy Spirit. Amen." I hop up, smiling.

———

A Kaiser nurse takes a vial of my blood, and I cross my fingers as she walks away to test it. Holding my breath, I wait and watch her every move as she re-enters the room. I zoom in on her face, trying to read it.

She looks at me and says, "Yes. Your blood test confirms you're pregnant."

I inhale, jump out of the chair, and race off to Steve's building, heady with happiness. I walk into his building like my feet are a few inches off the ground. I open the door to his office, glad he is alone, and say, "I'm pregnant."

He grins a giant grin and rises to hug me, and we both hold each other tightly. We pull back, and I see both happiness and a touch of caution in his eyes.

Chapter Eleven

TIME BOMB

August 1985

THE NEXT MORNING, in my office at the end of a psychotherapy appointment with a new client, a familiar pain starts deep in my pelvis, and I hear that loud train barreling toward me. My anxiety rises as the pain begins to make this dull thud in regular pulses like a heart beating in my belly.

I feel blood drain from my face as reality hits me. My heart can't stop from sinking into a deep, dark well, but none of this shows on the outside. And it shouldn't.

I have a new client here who doesn't know me. What am I going to do? Torn between being proper around her so as not to alarm her and knowing I am in deep trouble, I wait a few minutes before acting. Since my outer shell of a body does not reveal the ticking time bomb inside me, I muster a smile, and since we are at the end of the session, I politely usher the new client out of my office.

This time I know what is happening. I must act quickly to outrun death.

I call Steve and tell him the bad news: "I'm having another ectopic pregnancy."

His slow, drawn-out "Oh, no" is so full of disappointment it breaks my heart.

In pain going from level four to five and rising, I cradle my middle, shuffle down the hall, and knock on my officemate's door.

Gene is an older balding man with an easygoing manner and is usually unflappable. But at this moment he looks at me with wide eyes. "You don't look good. What's the matter?"

I whisper, "Gene, take me to the hospital right now. I'm having an ectopic pregnancy."

He nods and grabs his hat and keys.

As we make our way out the door, I peek into the waiting room and find my next client who looks up from her magazine. She's been a client of mine for years, so I tell her the truth. "I have to go to the hospital. I'm pregnant and having complications."

Her eyes grow big with fear, and I swallow back my tears and bite my lip.

I hear Gene lock his office door and walk toward me jangling his car keys. We walk to his car in the garage, and I climb in carefully. I see a giant glaring clock in my head that will not be stopped. My body is a ticking time bomb, and that is all I can think about.

Gene tries for light chatter, which grates against my ears.

"Gene, thank you for driving me, but please, I need quiet."

Gene nods. "Of course, sorry."

I am glad I'm being assertive and plan to continue that attitude this time, this second time through this ordeal.

Twenty minutes later I am in the emergency room. I hurry to the check-in desk, sign in, and tell the clerk, "I'm having an ectopic pregnancy right now." I refuse to wait six hours in some unknown hell of pain like the first time. I know my tube will burst; it is just a matter of time.

The clerk looks up from her clipboard. "Sit down, and we will call you when we can."

As soon as they put me in an exam room, Steve rushes in. We hold each other tight and both sigh in sad resignation.

An hour later we look at the sonogram with Dr. Blakely. In a passive tone he tells us, "Since you are only five weeks along, no pregnancy can be seen. We did see a mass on your right side. It might be an ovarian cyst or an ectopic pregnancy. But you could also still have a uterine pregnancy. We just don't know at this moment."

When the doctor says, "uterine pregnancy," I hear a choir of angels tune their horns to play a new song of hope. I pray that this is a normal pregnancy and the pain is an indication of nothing more than severe cramps. Dr. Reinsch had said this remaining tube is clear, so maybe, just maybe, everything will be okay. Also, the throbbing pain has subsided, so I don't feel as alarmed. I am eager to jump tracks and join the hope train again.

Dr. Blakely says, "You can go home now. Get some rest and come back next week. We might get a clear picture by then."

I nod, but Steve doesn't hear the angels, nor has he changed trains. "Home?" he says. "But last time she almost died. Shouldn't we take care of this now?"

The doctor tilts his head. "Well, since we really don't know what it is, there is nothing to take care of. We can't do the laparotomy because, if you are pregnant, the procedure could endanger the fetus."

Endanger the fetus? Oh, no. I look the doctor square in the eyes. "So what do we do?"

"All you can do is wait and hope."

That is all I want to do. Besides, the pain is gone.

We go home, have dinner, and head to bed. But after a few hours, a throbbing pain in my side, like hot prickly needles that won't subside, wakes me up. It is level seven pain. Go down, go down, I beg the pain. I count my breaths. I pray. Okay, a four. Maybe it will go away. Then a six. Then a seven. I look at the clock. It's mocking me like the ticking inside me. Who is right, me and my hope that can outlast time? Or this clock? The cold clock reads 3:30 a.m., and a level eight pain forces my hand.

I push Steve's shoulder to wake him up. At 4 a.m., we drive back to the hospital, and again, I demand to be seen right away. As they place me in an exam room, my radar goes up. I remember the first ectopic where the ER doctor was not an OB-GYN and handled me roughly.

A female doctor walks in, and I ask, "Are you an OB-GYN?"

When she responds, "No," I say, "I'm sorry, I only want an OB-GYN."

She looks slightly annoyed, purses her lips, and says, "Dr. Morell is the OB-GYN on call. You can wait for him if you want to."

She leaves, but I am worried, recalling that it was Dr. Morrell who had sent me home seven months ago with pills to stop a bladder infection when what I actually had was an ectopic pregnancy.

For twenty minutes, I hold onto my cramping belly as pain fluctuates from level two, three, four to five, six, seven and back down again. Dr. Morell walks in.

I look him in the eye and tell him my truth. "Last time, you gave me the wrong diagnosis. Maybe you did not have enough information, but I feel skeptical about trusting you."

He takes a step back. His eyes blink, and his back straightens. He is able to take this feedback in. With a reassuring voice, as he examines me gently, he says, "Here are your three options. The aggressive option is a laparotomy now. The conservative option is to go home and wait for the Saturday evening results of the beta HCC to confirm or deny a uterine pregnancy. Or you can take the mid-road, a culdocentesis."

"What's that?"

"Well, it's a procedure where we insert a needle under the cervix to draw fluid from the cul de sac between the uterus and perineum to see if we find blood. Blood means you need the laparotomy now. Other fluid means an ovarian cyst. If we find nothing, it tells us nothing."

As these options swirl above my head, he speaks with emphasis. "The culdocentesis would hurt for two minutes and be over."

Hearing the word "hurt" makes me cringe.

Steve looks at me and says, "If you don't do it, then you run the risk of bleeding back home, which is forty-five minutes away from this hospital." Too far away to save my life if I hemorrhage.

I nod at Steve, who tells the doctor, "Go ahead and do the culdocentesis now."

I hold Steve's hand as the doctor does the quick procedure. He looks at his syringe and says, "There is no blood or other fluid, so this tells us nothing definitive."

I am frustrated that I have no answers, yet I hold on to the spark of hope that I might still have a uterine pregnancy.

———

I eat lightly in case I need to have surgery, and I mark my pelvic pain over time. I feel no pain for one full day, which buoys my spirit that all is well. Then, I awaken in the middle of the night with sharp stabbing pains in my side. Maybe a level four but short lasting, the kind of pain that's easy to deny if you don't want to believe it. And I don't want to believe it.

Pain comes and goes for a few hours along with my adamant spirit fighting for belief in a uterine pregnancy. Steve rubs my back and plays classical music for me. I vomit once, but then the pain subsides as I enjoy the comfort of the bed and the pressure of Steve's hand on my back. Through sleepy eyes, I look at the painting on my wall. The subject is a woman in a toga, reclining in a lush Greek courtyard. I imagine her saying with care, "Honey, this is too much pain. Go to the hospital." I turn the other way to ignore her and sleep until morning.

The ringing phone wakes me up. A concerned sounding Dr. Blakely warns, "Don't eat anything after noon today."

My voice speeds up as I ask questions. "Why? Do I need to have surgery? Did you see something on my lab results? Could I be having a ruptured ovarian cyst?"

He was firm and clear. "That is unlikely. I will call you later with your beta HCG results. If they double, you do have a uterine pregnancy. If they don't, you have an ectopic and will need a laparotomy."

I sigh. "Yeah. I hope not."

"I'm sorry, but we don't know anything for sure yet. Remember not to eat. We will call you tonight."

I hang up the phone, cross my fingers, then slump down on the couch with a heavy heart. I know this day will put me on pins and needles as I wait to see which way my future goes.

I need a friend and dial Michelle, who is a therapist buddy of mine with a calm manner and a knack for making me feel better. She comes into my house, offering a warm hug.

We sit down with tea and chat. "You are understandably worried," she says, "and I can see the tension in your shoulders." Michelle stands behind me and gives me a shoulder massage.

My tension softens as I try to make sense of what is happening to me. "Maybe it means I am being punished for using the Dalkon Shield when I was younger."

Michelle shakes her head. "You know, I don't think we are punished for what we do. I think we are here to learn from each experience."

I listen, and she continues. "What if you open yourself up to the spiritual part of this experience? What if you went with the pain, followed it? There might just be an opening that will make you feel connected to something larger."

I let her words soak in. They dissolve some of the guilt from my past. I like the idea that I am supposed to learn something and connect to something larger. Connect to what, I don't know yet, but it makes me feel less like I am being forced to walk bare-foot over burning coals. A kind of peace spreads throughout my body. I know I am on a fire walk but one that may lead me some-where I need to go.

Later that evening, I pull a roasted chicken out of the oven just as the phone rings. Steve and I look at each other big-eyed. I place the pan on the stove and stiffly sit down at the kitchen table. Steve stands next to me with his hand on my shoulder. We brace ourselves for the promised diagnosis.

I let the doctor speak first. His voice is matter of fact. "So, here is what we have found out. Your values had been at thirty-five hundred. Values have to double, so that means they have to be at seven thousand for a uterine pregnancy."

I write that number on a yellow piece of paper, hoping the next number he utters will be at least seven thousand. I tighten my grip on the pencil, frozen in space.

"But they are only fifty-seven hundred."

As I repeat the dreaded number aloud, Steve grips my shoulder and says, "Oh, no."

I stare at the numbers as my pencil trails off the paper. I picture the machine that compresses cars in the junkyard, like I am a car about to be crushed. I ask the doctor, "How definite is that?"

"Well, your chance of a uterine pregnancy is 10 to 20 percent, and your chance of an ectopic is 80 percent."

I try to take it in—the 80 percent. I flatten into nothing. I vaguely hear the doctor summon us to the hospital immediately for a laparotomy. I know the drill. Before going totally into shock, Steve and I take a moment and look into each other's eyes to summon strength and prepare ourselves for the inevitable surgery. In a daze we drag ourselves to the car and drive silently to the hospital.

The surgeon, Dr. O'Patry, states, "I do not think you have enough clinical symptoms for surgery, and maybe you should wait."

I am taken aback. What? We have girded ourselves for this return sentence in hell because, even though we know the terrible drill, I don't want to die. What new twist is this? I feel jerked around. Do they know what they're doing? Maybe not.

Three doctors go into a huddle as I lie on the exam table. There is some back and forth until one of them turns toward me and says, "We all agree that you can wait."

"Wait? I'm confused. Why was I called to the hospital for surgery? Why aren't we doing the surgery now?" I feel pushed up and down and around as if on a roller coaster that makes me grip the wheel, and I hope my head doesn't snap from the sharp turns.

"We don't have clinical evidence, meaning we can't see an ectopic growing outside the uterus. So we think you need more time to be sure. Come back tomorrow for another sonogram."

What can I say? No, do the surgery now, so I don't feel jerked around anymore? But that admits defeat and total surrender. I shake my head, and I know it's crazy but I hold onto a little bud of hope—that slim 10 to 20 percent chance that my pregnancy might still be okay.

Steve looks at the doctor. "So you are saying we should go home?"

As they nod yes, I grab Steve's sleeve. "I am too scared to go back home because we will be an hour away from this hospital." Anxiety rises inside me. "We need to stay closer in case I have a rupture." I think back to what happened the first time. We call some friends who live near the hospital and ask if we can spend the night.

As we drive to their house I try to wipe away an image that haunts me—the image of explosives strapped to my body and about to go off anytime.

I try to sleep.

Chapter Twelve

FIERY ANGER

THE NEXT MORNING, I throw up while trying to drink water in the car as Steve drives me back to the hospital.

Steve joins me in the exam room where nurse Clarissa prepares me for a sonogram.

I stare at her placid face, trying to read it as she chews gum and moves the wand over my belly. She squints, sighs, and pops that damn gum like a carefree kid skipping at a playground. Snapping gum like nothing important is happening, like she isn't about to possibly reveal the death of our dream. We follow her every movement in slow motion. She turns, and we look up into her eyes as if our lives depend on whatever she says next. I can't wait any longer.

I beg, "Please tell us."

She shrugs her shoulders and shakes her head. "No, I can't. We are supposed to wait for the radiologist."

I frown. "Clarissa, we need to know. Please."

She stops chewing, shrugs again, and whispers, "I see an ectopic pregnancy lodged in the tube, and there is no uterine pregnancy."

As if we are riding the roller coaster shoulder to shoulder, Steve and I plummet into an emotional nosedive. Heavy sadness adds fifty pounds to my back. I look at Steve. His gaze seems far away as he spaces out, and then he looks crushed.

The radiologist enters, does not make eye contact with either of us, looks at the screen, and says coldly, "Yes, I confirm an ectopic pregnancy. Get dressed and go back to the waiting room. Your doctor will call you."

He and Clarissa walk out without another word. *Without a word.* Without any acknowledgment that they've just handed us tragic news. The rollercoaster they operated has crashed, and all the people on it were killed. And they just walked away with a shrug.

A fire of outrage rises throughout my body. As I get dressed, I tell Steve, "Oh, no. They can't treat us like this. We need to find somewhere to be alone."

Steve, who often goes along with authority, nods in agreement.

We find a bathroom in the hallway, go in together, and lock the door. Steve's belly wobbles as he begins to cry. That makes me cry. Steve pulls me close and holds me tighter than he ever has as I sob loudly.

After this needed time as a couple to express our grief, we return and sit in the waiting room. Too soon, a nurse calls our names. As I enter the exam room, the first thing I see is a giant poster of a smiling pregnant woman holding her full belly. She is everything I want to be and just learned I will never be.

My anger boils over, and I lose it. I walk toward the poster, raise my hands like lion claws, and imagine ripping it off the wall. I want to use all this fire inside to do some damage. But I know it's wrong.

Clarissa walks in. Unable to put out the flame of my quick-moving fire, I turn it on her. "You people gave us bad news and no time to react. You just walked out. Leave us alone. Get out of here. We need time alone."

She raises her eyebrows and swiftly leaves. Steve grabs me by the shoulders, pulls me in, and puts his hand on the top of my head. The fire slowly cools as I exhale and calm down. I may not have been fair to Clarissa. I knew she had done me a favor, and I should've respected that instead of blaming her for the news. It wasn't her fault that she saw what she saw. Still, I couldn't stop my anger from ramping up. I would've torn that whole place down if I'd had the strength.

About five minutes later, Dr. Blakely enters the room. His smile seems out of place. He must know about the ectopic. Why is he smiling? Another medical person who doesn't have the basic humanity to be with us in our bad news. A wave of nausea hits me as his first words are, "Can you lie back? I would like to examine you."

I do not lie back.

I can't even believe he is asking. "Why? What more do you need to know?"

He looks taken aback, unsure what to do next. "Well, okay. Why don't you get dressed and meet me in my office."

Within ten minutes we sit across from Dr. Blakely and his large oak desk. He shuffles papers around, as if he wants to move on to the next thing: scheduling the surgery.

I am still swimming in the experience and need him to know. "Doctor, how can you tell us devastating news and not provide a moment for us to react? This is wrong. You people need to change that."

He looks at me like I am a burden, shuffles his papers again, and sighs, "Oh, okay, um well, Dr. O'Patry will do your surgery at nine tonight."

It hits me that he lives in some other universe, a universe without compassion. I see that he is unable to do anything other than state facts. I walk away, shaking my head, distressed that some medical people don't seem to care about the patient as a person.

Since we have three or four hours to wait, Steve turns toward me. "Let's get out of here, go outside, and talk on the grass."

The bright green grass next to the hospital looks soft, smells sweet, and invites us to lie down. The grass cushions my back, the sun warms my face, and the pepper trees sway gently below the sparse clouds. Here, time slows, grass grows, and there is relief from being quickly ushered to the next procedure by white coats. The green grass is giving us oxygen, enough oxygen to quiet my spirit and let my anger float away like a leaf in the wind. As my anger subsides, a shiver of fear takes its place. My baby is growing in the wrong place again. It will not survive.

I turn to Steve. "Why is this happening again?"

He shakes his head. "It doesn't seem fair." He reaches over and squeezes my hand as I look at clouds that promise some kind of softness that doesn't seem to exist inside the sterile hospital. Yet that sterile place is the only place where they can save me.

Chapter Thirteen

SONIC BOOM

August 1985

HOURS before the scheduled surgery of my second ectopic pregnancy, I close my eyes, take a long breath and pray, "God, please help me accept this thing I cannot change."

Steve whimpers and shakes.

I reach out to hold him, and his chest shudders rapidly against mine as he sobs. After some tears, we get up and take a long hand-in-hand walk around the grounds. I see one lone white-and-yellow plumeria blossom on a dark green bush. I lean over and inhale its sweet pungent scent before we reenter the hospital.

An antiseptic scent rises as we walk up to the admission desk.

The clerk states, "It will be another hour before your bed is ready."

We are back in the land of being told what to do and when. I can't eat due to the upcoming surgery, but Steve is hungry, so we amble, sad-eyed, toward the nearly empty cafeteria.

As soon as Steve returns to the table and takes a bite of his sandwich, a sharp level nine pain rips through my left side. My skin goes cold and clammy, and I feel another sonic boom of pain. I am nauseated, and my head swims sideways like I'm going to faint. I think I might be bleeding internally. I can almost hear Dr. O'Patry's voice in my head: *"If your fallopian tube bursts, you will fill with blood. Blood will fill your pelvic cavity, rise, and fill your chest cavity."* I know that, if this is what's happening, I might die.

My brain becomes woozy, but fear presses me to stay alert. I tell Steve, "Go get me a wheelchair."

He drops his sandwich and runs off to find one.

I push down my rising terror as my heart sinks. My chin quivers to fight back tears. I take a deep breath.

The female nurse who preps me for emergency surgery pronounces my name correctly. This means everything to me.

"Thank you for pronouncing my name right," I say.

She pats my shoulder as we make our way into the OR, and she says, "I am Phillipina. I can pronounce your beautiful name."

The doors close. My life is in the doctors' hands as they rush to save me. Before I go under, I take back time because there is only this moment, which might be my last. I tell God, "If this is the end of my life, I want to thank you for my three years with Steve. I love him so much. I'm sorry for any pain I have caused others. Thank you for my family and watch over all of them."

Chapter Fourteen

POST-SURGERY

Wax Candle

I OPEN MY EYES, my head clears quickly, and I see Steve standing above me. His loving eyes warm my heart.

I have not died.

But I am still a failure. I know the baby is gone. I tell Steve, "I am so sorry this happened."

He cuts me off. "No, don't say that. This isn't your fault."

Dr. O'Patry walks into the room. As he checks my bandage and lungs, I ask, "How long was the operation?"

"Thirty minutes." He moves to the side of the bed and looks at me seriously. "I tried to save the tube, but it was bleeding profusely, and it was impossible to save."

I cringe.

He looks away for a moment, as if remembering, then snaps back. "I wanted to cut a wedge that later could be put together, but I couldn't. I had to cut across the fimbria."

No more fallopian tubes feels like castration. This means utter failure. Inside I am melting like a wax candle, burning and sliding away from myself, completely slipping away from my dream of ever giving birth.

———

Later that day, a young social worker in a smart blue suit, with brown hair in a tight bun, walks in holding a clipboard.

I sit up in bed, grateful for the space to talk, and tell her, "I have so many feelings about what just happened."

She stands at the foot of my bed, nods, and says, "Well, let's look at your future." Her cool manner stuns me.

I was getting used to most of the medical staff being cold and jumping to the next procedure without taking a beat, but this is someone in my field. We are trained to listen. I feel like a therapy supervisor challenging her to be more present, so I give her another chance.

"I am so sad that I lost another baby . . . I was terrified when they wheeled me into surgery . . . and broken-hearted that they couldn't save my fallopian tube."

She looks at her chart. "You should consider in vitro fertilization."

Somehow, having just survived this second brush with death and surgery has given me a thicker skin, and I don't feel as fragile. I know she won't process feelings like I want her to, so I decide to follow her road for a while.

"What? Ah, no, that is too expensive for us."

She presses on. "Ten thousand dollars is reasonable."

Is she rich? Money is no object? I look at the scar on my stomach. It is red and angry and only a few hours old.

I look into her eyes, searching for some hint of understanding, but find none. I give up and respond, "In vitro is not covered by insurance. It's elective."

She scours her chart for a moment. "Well, ten thousand dollars doesn't seem too prohibitive. A Porsche costs twenty thousand dollars."

A *Porsche?* Does she drive one? We are comparing Porsches to IVF? At this point, I secretly smile from how dense she is. If she were a student, and I were her teacher in a psychology course, I would fail her on this lesson. Since she isn't helpful or kind, I want her to leave.

I stare at her. "Look, I'm not ready to consider that and don't have that kind of money."

She shrugs like she thinks she did her job well, hands me a card for Kaiser psychiatric care, and walks out the door.

Chapter Fifteen

TURTLES

WHEN THE NIGHT COMES, I look out my hospital room window at a dark vast sky that goes off into a mysterious somewhere. Where are the answers? I clench my fists that still belong to my body. I can feel them at the ends of my arms. I clench them in rhythm, just because I can. Unlike my excavated insides, which are now a mysterious dark hole.

I don't feel whole.

After I toss and turn for hours, the sunlight breaks through the window, and Dr. Morell enters my room, ready to wrap things up.

I ask him why my tubes were scarred.

He is crisp. "Well, very likely, the Dalkon Shield that you used caused pelvic inflammatory disease, which can cause scarring. Do you recall being in pain after it was inserted?"

"Yes, I was doubled over in pain for the first week. When I walked, it felt like hot pokers were stabbing my lower belly. I went to the doctor to ask if the shield was the problem, and he told me to leave it in and try it for a month."

"Oh, I know this is hard to hear, but that is most likely why. Pelvic inflammatory disease can cause permanent fallopian tube scarring, which results in infertility."

My heart sinks to the bottom of my belly and falls all the way through the floor. I think back to when I had the Dalkon Shield inserted. Oh, my God, why did I do it? How stupid was that? And why didn't I take it out when I first had pain? Why did I trust them when they said it was safe?

I am brought back into the room by the sound of the doctor's clipboard. He says, "With ectopics, we used to routinely remove the uterus and ovaries. But you can still become a mother, you know."

I nod, but I'm still lost in a puddle.

"You know, we haven't perfected it, and there are risks, but we could talk about in vitro."

I both want to hear what he is saying and I want him to stop talking altogether—my body is still reeling from a fresh wound.

I begin cautiously, "Yeah, the social worker mentioned something about that. I don't know much about it." I feel an ounce of interest and ask, "I'm not ready for it, but does it work? What are the dangers?"

"They give you a drug called Pergonal, which makes your body produce extra eggs. After ten days of injections, we retrieve about three-to-six eggs through laparoscopy. We fertilize the eggs in a petri dish, then transfer the eggs into your uterus. As far as dangers go, it's all pretty new, but you can have multiple births or lose the pregnancies and have complications, such as low birth weight."

This is too much information, which swims in my head. I heard "laparoscopy" and "lose the pregnancies."

I look up at him with a sudden firmness. "No thanks—not now anyway."

After he leaves, I think about my body with its missing parts. It hits me hard that my body can never get pregnant naturally. My thoughts swirl into a spiral that goes from chaos to some semblance of order. My body has been through too much and needs a rest. I can't put myself through anymore.

A door closes. In my chest, I feel a surge of golden heat that surrounds my heart. Something begs to be heard. My heart starts to beat to the rhythm of a new drum. It gets so loud it shouts in my ear, "I want a baby in my arms and I want it now!"

I follow this new surge of energy as it travels briskly and turns in a new direction, leading me to a bright new view of life, a new path to make my dream come true.

I ring for a nurse like it is a medical necessity. When she walks in, I look at her firmly. "I want to adopt. What do I need to do?"

The nurse runs off and returns with a handful of pamphlets from local adoption agencies and puts them in my hands. I fan them out before me, and my eyes fill with excitement, as if these pamphlets are the first steps on that new path.

A few hours later, I am abuzz when Steve walks in and sits down in the hard hospital chair. His eyes seem vacant, his shoulders slump over, and he stares at his hands.

I show him the pamphlets. He holds them loosely, barely taking them in, then nods weakly and asks, "Can we take a walk?" I swallow my enthusiasm about the new road and follow him.

———

We move slowly down the pale green hallways. The hospital is eerily quiet.

After a few minutes he speaks up. "I feel depressed and pissy. Driving here tonight, I fantasized about running people off the road."

His jaw tightens, and his eyes squint. Steve is usually slow to anger, so this stuns me. As we walk, he notices the door is open to the exam room where we had our last ultrasound, the one where they saw that the pregnancy was in the tube. We peek in.

Steve says, "We could go in there and smash that sonogram machine."

I widen my eyes, feeling drawn to join him in doing violence to that which took away our dream. We crane our necks to peek farther, but our feet stay glued outside that room of doom. We pull our heads out and turn away silently as our fire cools down. As we walk, I look over at Steve's face. His eyes switch from angry daggers to pools of sorrow and his chin quivers. He is frowning and drowning all at once, and it hurts me to see him in so much pain. My heart wants to jump out and enfold him, and I place a hand on his back. We both sigh—that kind of heavy sigh that marks a giving in to destiny.

These ectopics make us lose our protective shell, that sense of immunity we had as a young couple. We are now two shell-less turtles, fragile, slow walking in shock.

Chapter Sixteen

NEW MISSION

WHEN WE GET HOME from the hospital, the heavy weight of the finality of our infertility fills this once hope-filled space. As I look around the front room, one part of me drops in sorrow while another part of me wants to stay open to the idea of adoption.

I drop my bag and sit at the kitchen table, looking through the mail. I open a condolence card from Steve's teenage stepsister. Her message reads, "Your loss is tragic, and my heart goes out to you. You may want to consider adoption. As an adoptee, I feel very special . . ."

I hold the letter and think about her, picture her smile and think about the adoption option. Somewhere out there is a child we can raise. Steve and I would be great parents. I feel a new sensation as a deep desire rises in my chest. In my mind's eye, I see a tight little rosebud slowly blossom into a full pink flower with petals that look like cupped hands softly opening.

Who would that baby be? Would he or she look like us? Does that matter? Where would he or she come from? I feel some anxiety, but mostly, I feel as if a door I never knew existed has unlocked itself and is inviting me into a new room. I want to take a step inside, but first, I look down at my body. It has endured too much. I look at my belly. My body is done. Did all it could. I can't make a baby on my own, and I can't handle any more doctors or invasions to this body. I've come too close to death.

And we have been stripped of our armor and exposed to raw pain from our baby losses.

I just want to live. But I want to live in a world with a baby I can raise. A baby some other woman carries and births but can't provide for on her own for some reason. A baby she entrusts Steve and me to care for. Because we are ready. Ready to love fully without hesitation or doubt.

My engines rev with more power as I head up this imaginary hill. Yes, love without conditions or ambivalence. Love that will be here for the ride as we climb to the heavens in thrilling highs, and here for the ride if we descend into devastating lows.

In my reverie I talk directly to our baby-to-be and say, "We hold on to each other, and we will hold on to you and cover you with the blanket of our love all your life."

———

Over dinner I look at Steve, and with resolution in my voice, I say, "I am ready for adoption."

Steve looks at me warmly. "Me too."

The next day, I plunge in. I am both nervous and excited as I dial the number for county adoptions.

The woman who answers the phone sounds enthusiastic about our prospects and says, "You sound like the kind of couple we look for as adoptive parents."

I gasp, inhaling a chest full of desire. I want to be "the kind of couple" they look for. I am on a new mission. I put the blinders on and forge ahead, not pausing to learn much about the world of adoption with all its factors and possible issues. I am racing my racehorse, leaning forward, as the trees rush by in a verdant blur. I don't pause to look and see what I don't want to see.

The receptionist at county adoptions asks, "Do you want to receive the paperwork to start the process?"

I shout, "Yes!" Then, I quickly ask what information they will need from us.

She is upbeat. "Well, we want to know who you are and how you live. We want to see the nature of your closeness and stability."

I hang up the phone with my insides fluttering. I check the mailbox every day for a week until the forms finally arrive.

As soon as I pull the package out of the mailbox, I tear it open and get started. Steve and I spread the application forms out on the kitchen table. I am eager to make us look like we would be good parents. It seems like they want to know everything about us—careers, length of marriage, where we live, how we live, hobbies, extended family, community, support, parenting style, medical history, religion, and ethnicity. I write as fast as I can.

Steve dictates details about his work as an ecologist who studies the kelp forest, and I write about my career as a psychotherapist. In terms of lifestyle, I write, "We love bird-watching, playing tennis, and going to the beach. We are devoted to each other, we love our work, and we are best friends."

On a more personal note, I add, "Raising a family is something we both want very much. Unfortunately, we cannot have our own. I had two ectopic pregnancies, one in January 1985 and one in August 1985. In our longing to be parents, we wish to offer our hearts and our home to a child we can adopt."

A wave sweeps through me—the fluttering of possibility. I put down my pen. My chest lifts as I think about us meeting their standards. I know we are good candidates, and we are ready. I can almost feel the weight as I imagine holding a baby in my arms.

I drift off to sleep smiling about adoption but wake up with a gripping sensation. A fierce pelvic cramp makes me double over.

I go to the bathroom, sit on the toilet, and urinate. As I wipe myself, there is a large clump on the paper. *What is this?*

I feel alarm and fascination as I see what looks like human tissue. I touch it and hold it up to the light. It looks like skin, strong, sturdy, and very thin. I whisper, "Is this part of the placenta? . . . Part of the baby?" I put it in the toilet, pause, then flush and hear a gushing sound, a sound I've heard a million times before, but it shocks me. I stare as it swirls away to oblivion.

I go back to bed somberly, in a daze, as if I am returning from a funeral. I toss and turn and look at the ceiling. I'm pretty sure I know the truth—that this is the last of my pregnancy. Some medical person somewhere along the line must have said that some dense tissue discharge after baby loss was "to be expected."

I don't need to know the truth.

I tell Steve in the morning. He looks at me with sad eyes and touches my hand. It's over; that was the final remnant. There is nothing more to say or do.

———

A few days later, I open my door to find my older sister, Peggy, smiling with her big, kind eyes and long, curly brown hair, holding her suitcase. She has flown in from Sacramento with a mission to be with me in this early post-ectopic era. As we hug, my whole body relaxes.

After breakfast, Peggy takes my hand and says, "Let's go to the salon today, and you can get a nice haircut."

My body is still weak, two weeks post-hospital stay, and I feel reluctant to leave the house, but Peggy puts me in the car, turns on her favorite reggae music, and Bob Marley sings to me, reminding me not to worry about a thing.

Chapter Seventeen

THE HAIRCUT

I HAVE BEEN ENSCONCED indoors and on a seesaw of mixed emotions, teetering down in baby-loss grief, then up in adoption excitement. As we drive to the salon, I look out the car window and squint at the bright sun of the world. I am not sure I can handle anything else, even with Bob Marley trying to soothe me with his song. I give it a try. I take breath, look at Peggy, run my fingers through my long brown locks, and say, "I like my long hair. Just a trim, right?"

"Sure. Don't worry, even a small change can shift your whole perspective!"

I look at her confident big-sister smile and nod in semi-agreement. My body is tired, and my mind is introverted and reluctant to follow anything else new. But maybe all I need is a little shift in perspective.

A half-hour later I sit in a pure white boutique salon with tall windows and large mirrors. I vaguely hear people speaking around me—something about a brand-new hairstylist who is going to cut my hair.

My sister takes a seat and opens a magazine. The hairstylist pulls out her scissors and gets started. I sit in a big, black, cushioned chair, feeling spacey and lost in time, paying no attention.

I am a seagull flying over the ocean who doesn't want to dip down and peer into the water of real life. A buzzing sound brings me back to earth. I look at myself in the mirror. I'm in shock. My hair is gone. It is shaped into a super short pixie cut. It reminds me of my brothers' crew cuts from when we were kids.

Pleased with herself, the hairdresser turns my chair around, hands me a mirror, and proudly asks, "How do you like the wedge I created? It is the newest style."

I look at the floor, and, strewn around beneath my feet are the strands of my long brown hair. Parts of me I didn't ask to lose, now dead on the ground. I look in the mirror again and notice a triangular chunk shaved out of the back of my head.

I look like a boy. I look like a boy right after I've learned I can never give birth! This haircut is like wearing a sign exposing me as a fraud to all the world. Unfeminine, infertile.

"Oh, my God." I want to scream, but I am too horrified to say more.

My sister looks up from her magazine, noticing the commotion. She rushes over to me.

"Peggy, my hair is all gone, what did they do to me?"

My sister puts her hand over her mouth and frowns at the hairstylist. "She didn't ask for that. What did you do?"

Unphased, the hairstylist quips, "She wasn't saying much of anything, and I think it looks good."

I touch the back of my naked neck with prickly short hairs. A wedge. The same word the doctor used: "I had to cut a wedge . . ."

I want to yell but feel the same powerlessness I often felt in the hospital. Stroking the top of my head, I shiver. No longer hidden on the inside, my infertility now shows on the outside.

I am naked. There's nowhere to hide. I stare at my face in the mirror to keep from detaching into invisibility. Here are my round eyes, saucers of shock but still hazel. Still here. Still mine. Here are my cheekbones; here is my chest, rising and falling in a breath.

Let me breathe slowly and blink to go from blurry-focused to clear enough to get up. I stand, but my legs are wobbly like rubber. I lean on one leg and wait until the weight goes all the way to my foot. Then, I lean on the other leg. I find my feet, press them into the ground, take a step away from here. I can't wait to get away.

I tell the owner about the bad haircut. He apologizes and offers to fix my hair, but he can't. You can't put something back once it's been cut away. The damage is done.

As I walk to the car, I picture those long, dead locks of wavy brown hair lying on the white tile floor being swept up by a broom and tossed in the garbage bin.

Peggy drives us home as I fall into my inner world. This bad haircut I never asked for is just another someone with a blade who decided to cut away pieces of me as if it was no big deal. As if it was up to them because they said so. The hairdresser is like the doctors who've had their hands on me, in me, taking what doesn't belong to them in the interest of making me "better," doing what's "right," what needs to be done. Not asking me, not letting me be whole anymore.

My long hair as a child set me apart from the twins who were one year older with their short pixie haircuts. I was one of seven sisters, but I was the only one with long braids. This helped me feel distinctive in a sea of similar faces.

Then, Mom cut my braids. I was sheared then too, shaved away without my permission. Defeminized, dehumanized, invisible.

Chapter Eighteen

PENGUINS

THE FOLLOWING NIGHT, Steve and Peggy take me to SeaWorld. They hope seeing the penguins and the whale and dolphin shows with cheery music might help me feel better.

Steve rents a wheelchair for me because I am only a few weeks into recovery from surgery and I lack energy. I can only stand for ten minutes at a time, but I don't like the idea of needing a wheelchair, so I say, "I will push it myself and only sit in it when I get tired."

Steve pulls out the wheelchair and tells me to sit. "Look, when you get tired, you get grumpy. Then, no one can have fun." I am taken aback by this comment but agree to his plan.

Being pushed over a wooden bridge is rocky and makes my stitches hurt. People give me stiff smiles and subtly look to see if my limbs are shriveled. In the bathroom I have trouble maneuvering but feel grateful for help and an accessible stall. This new view from a chair makes me vow to be more sensitive to others who, unlike me, may need to use a chair permanently.

I have lost my hair, which dampens my spirit, but the sting will wear off eventually. The hair will grow back, and I can look as feminine as I want to in the future.

At the crowded penguin encounter, standing people block

my sitting view. They don't seem to notice or accommodate. I crane my neck to see penguins in family units.

Steve and I look up at a video that shows both parents incubating their young, and we watch penguin eggs hatch. The video's narrator says, "The first penguin born outside Antarctica was born in San Diego in 1980."

I tell Steve, "Even penguins out of their environment can breed—but not us."

He says, "I was thinking the same thing." As he grabs the handles to push my wheelchair, he mumbles, "We are like genetic dead ends."

I startle at the harshness of his words.

Chapter Nineteen

QUICK FIX

THE NEXT DAY, I wake up feeling a sense of resolve. I ask Peggy to play "Out-Out-Out" with me. It is the name our family gave to the process of having another person help you go through your closet to thin out your wardrobe.

I fill a few bags as Peggy chooses a silk blouse, black tunic, mauve top, and a few skirts for herself.

"I have one more thing you might like." I reach into the back of my closet and pull out a long, brown satin-and-lace maternity dress with lots of volume below the empire waist. I had picked out the fabric and commissioned a seamstress to make it back in my hippie days in San Francisco.

Peggy looks at it up and down. "That is beautiful."

I touch the smooth satin ribbon and twirl the dress around.

"I have saved this for ten years, for one purpose. I wanted to wear it when I was pregnant."

Peggy drops her hands in her lap, looks at me, and says, "I'm so sorry."

I hand it to her across the bed. She takes the dress, holds it to her chest, and looks at me with eyes that wish they could erase my sorrow. She folds the dress to add to her pile.

Later, aware that I am adjusting to a new normal, I read through an adoption pamphlet.

I pick up my yellow legal pad and look at my adoption to-do list. The first task is to ask anyone around me if they can point me in the right direction.

I call Steve's father, who is a doctor in Santa Cruz, hoping he may have some pointers. I say, "I wonder if you might know someone in your hospital who is planning to put their baby up for adoption."

He is supportive and offers to talk to his hospital connections and get back to me. This feels promising, and I surf a wave of hopefulness that gives me a burst of energy. If I dive full force—and quickly—into this, maybe I can stay on the surfboard all the way to shore without falling off. I don't slow down long enough to see if the sea has any rip currents. A successful ride is all I can allow my mind to fathom.

Next, I open the yellow pages of the phonebook and let my index finger scroll under the letter "A" until I find a series of ads. The first one reads, "Adoption Facilitation Services"; another reads, "Alternative Pregnancy Care Clinic"; and one advertises, "Quick and Easy Adoptions." A rush of excitement scurries past any concern that maybe this won't be "quick and easy."

I call Quick and Easy Adoptions.

An eager lawyer answers and jumps right in. "We handle independent adoptions. That means we get calls every day from pregnant women seeking good homes for their babies."

I gasp, picturing a revolving door of women like me going in empty-handed and coming out with a baby. I can barely contain myself and blurt out, "How does this work, exactly?" The salesman has found his mark. And I naïvely enter his lair.

He speaks with confidence. "A pregnant woman, or her parents, contacts us to arrange an adoption between two parties. This is the fastest way to get a baby. Fees vary, but adoptive parents usually pay all the costs."

I brush aside any concern about money, at least for the moment.

"How many babies do you have? I mean, how quickly could this happen?"

"The demand is larger than the supply in the USA. Foreign adoptions are more complex than in-country adoptions."

"What is the difference between independent adoption and agency adoption?"

"In independent adoptions, like we do here, the wait is usually six-to-nine months, and you arrange it on your own. If you go with an agency, the wait will most likely be around two years."

A jolt of electricity pushes me toward this private route. I don't think I can wait two years.

His next sentence gives me pause. "Something you should know is that, in a private adoption, the birth mom changes her mind in 10 to 25 percent of the cases."

I am surfing over rip currents I don't want to feel. "But 75 to 90 percent of the time, it works, right?"

"Oh, absolutely. You need an attorney, and you may be able to bond with the baby right in the hospital after it's born. You should also know that, in all types of adoption, they send a social worker to your house for a home study, to assess the suitability of the environment."

"Okay, thank you," I say, practically mooning over the phrase "bond with the baby." Then, I ask a question I don't know if I want the answer to. "I'm also wondering, what is the level of involvement of the birth parents after the adoption?"

"Well, agencies are getting more flexible. They used to only allow closed adoption, where the records on the identity of the birth parents are sealed and you would have no interaction with them at all. Now, some agencies allow 'open' adoption, where the identities of the birth parents and adoptive parents are known to both parties. And sometimes the birth parents are involved in some way."

I take in his words. Involved? How involved? I imagine a birth mother standing on a playground with us and our toddler. My neck tenses up as fear spreads through me. I want to raise the child with Steve only. I want to cling to my vision of the three of us tightly bonded. I don't want a birth mother in our lives. I am aware that I am pushing away another person, that I am not ready to consider her and her world. Not yet. Maybe never. And I am aware that my baby may want to know where he or she came from.

But I can only fit the three of us in this small box, and I won't let my mind consider letting another mother in. I fear that, if she climbs in the box with us somehow, the cardboard will begin to bend, tear, and collapse, leaving us lost and exposed. All I know is that my narrowly focused, uninformed adoptive-parent-mind is scared and protective.

———

A few weeks later, I wake up in a panic and look at the clock. "Oh, my God! It's my first day back. I forgot!"

I pick up the phone to call my client. No answer. Still unable to drive because it hurts my insides, I turn to Steve. "Can you take me to the office?"

Steve, who gets to airports two to three hours ahead even for domestic flights, looks worried. "What? You should have reminded me. You will never make it on time! Your office is forty-five minutes away."

"I know, but please. She is supposed to be my first client. I can't not show up." I throw on my clothes, and he rushes me out the door.

Steve's car screeches up to the curb, and I tumble out. I am ten minutes late. Still drowsy from getting up earlier than usual and flustered from having to rush, I make my way over to a brown-haired woman in a long dress, who is waiting patiently on the office steps. I feel a wave of embarrassment as I reach her.

For a moment, we regard one another. It hits me that the last time I saw her I was running out this door facing an ectopic pregnancy I'd worried might kill me.

As I usher her inside, she catches me up on her life. She too had just had a life-threatening experience. "I had a blood clot in my lung. It almost killed me."

I look deeply into the eyes of someone who has shared a similar nightmare and find myself saying, without thinking, "Well, we are both alive!"

She nods her head with the gravity of someone who has recently stared into the abyss. She smiles and says, "We sure are!"

After our session, she reaches out and hugs me warmly, pulls back, and says, "This is the hug I wanted to give you four weeks ago when I was in the waiting room and you had to be rushed to the hospital."

I gasp as tears sting my eyes. We are two souls joined in the commonality of near-death resonance. I could have died. She could have died. My fetus died, but we are alive and meant to go on. As a therapist I usually focus on the world of the client, but this time, she and I helped heal each other.

Chapter Twenty

POSTPARTUM

ONE EVENING after we've both had long days at work, Steve walks into the kitchen while I toss a salad. He opens the garbage can lid with his foot. "I don't need these anymore." He sounds resigned and tosses blue boxes of condoms in the trash. I look up into his droopy hound-dog eyes. We eat dinner in somber silence.

After dinner, I tear open an envelope from Kaiser Hospital. It's an appointment reminder, in large black letters, for a postpartum check-up. "It's time to check on you and the new baby!"

I feel a stab in the heart as anger rises in my body.

I dial Kaiser. "Hey, you sent me a postpartum check-up notice. I had an ectopic pregnancy!"

"Oh, I am so sorry," says the clerk on night duty. "We made a mistake."

I hang up on her, tear the note into pieces, toss them in the garbage, and watch the small white strips land on the boxes of useless condoms.

It's all too much. I pull off my apron, ball it up, and throw it onto the table. My eyes tear up, and I lie on the couch and sink into sadness.

When Steve turns on the television, I go to the bedroom to be alone. I lie on the bed and close my eyes, and scenes from funerals come to mind. Some unfamiliar force pulls at me until I feel a clear urge to create some type of "postpartum" memorial. I return to the living room and tell Steve, "I have to do something to mark our losses."

He raises his eyebrows, then returns to the TV.

In the garage, I rifle through old Easter decorations. I grab one pink and one blue plastic egg, the kind you fill with candy. I create two tiny makeshift coffins. Around each egg coffin, I use Scotch tape to attach paper on which I write would-be baby names. I take them into the small backyard, dig two shallow holes under the grass, and place them in the dirt. Dusting the soil from my hands, I inhale its moist earthy scent. After staring at the graves for a while, I go inside to get Steve. "Can you come outside and join me in a ceremony?"

He doesn't want to leave his program but turns it off, gets up from his chair with a hesitant look on his face, comes outside, and finds the burial spot. The hollow look in his eyes says he doesn't want to be here.

I say a prayer of goodbye as I cover the tiny oblong graves, replace the green grass, and give our dream babies to the earth.

My heart dives into the graves with them, and I can't move. I don't ever want to move. Steve puts his arm around me, and we both stand there frozen, staring at the ground.

Chapter Twenty~One

EMPTY CRADLE

I SIT NEXT to a pregnant young woman in the doctor's waiting room. She's wearing a corduroy maternity jumper and cheerfully crocheting yellow baby booties.

When my name is called, I follow the curly-haired nurse to the exam room. It has been six weeks since the surgery. As I take a seat on the exam table, the nurse looks at me with compassion, holds my gaze, and says, "I'm so sorry you can't have children."

I swallow the lump in my throat.

Dr. O'Patry, who performed both my ectopic surgeries, enters the room. He puts on his gloves, examines me, and offers a smile. "It looks good. Your scar will shrink to only a few inches and will barely be perceptible."

Relieved to hear that this large scar that spans from one hip to the other will shrink, I dress and walk into his wood-paneled office. As I take a seat in front of his large oak desk, I notice photos of children on the wall behind him. "Is that your family?"

His eyes smile. "Yes, I have a wife and six children."

I sigh and say exactly what I'm thinking. "I am sad that I can't have any of my own."

He leans back in his chair and raises his eyebrows. "I know, but they turn into teenagers, you know. My thirteen-year-old just broke his arm playing baseball. Believe me, children are a lot of hard work and heartache."

Another disconnect. How many people before me must have sat in this office after baby loss? Did he really think he was saying something helpful?

His words make me think of a conversation between the Wizard and the Tin Man in *The Wizard of Oz*. The Wizard says, "Hearts will never be practical until they can be made unbreakable." The Tin Man looks at him and says, "But I . . . I still want one."

We know our hearts can break, we know kids' bones can break, but we still want one. We want to be parents. We want to raise children with our loving hearts.

As I drive home, I realize just how much I want to move on. I am still sad; a piece of my heart will always be bruised. But I feel myself shifting up again toward the hill of adoption. I make a detour on my drive home. At the city library, I ask the clerk to guide me to books on adoption.

I flip through material and find something interesting. I sit and read an article about a family who adopted two children after trying for four years to have their own. I look at the photo of this family with two smiling kids sitting on their parents' laps, and my heart lights up. Next, I pick up a book of poetry related to adoption and a touching poem by an unknown author calls to me:

The Legacy of Two Mothers

Once there were two women who never knew each other.

One you do not remember, the other you call Mother.

Two different lives shaped to make yours.

One became your guiding star; the other became your sun.

The first gave you life; the second taught you to live it.

The first gave you a need for love, and the second was there to give it.

One gave you a nationality; the other gave you a name.
One gave you the seed of talent; the other gave you aim.
One gave you emotions; the other calmed your fears.
One saw your first sweet smile; the other dried your tears.
One gave you up—it was all she could do.
The other prayed for a child, and God led her straight to you.
Now you ask through all your tears the age-old question
through the years:
Heredity or environment—which are you a product of?
Neither, my darling—neither—just two different kinds of
love.

I put the book down, my heart awakening. This is my first real
understanding that, someday, a birth mother will sacrifice a
piece of her heart and hand it to me.

Slowly, I read the poem again. Earlier, when I pictured a birth
mother at the playground with us and our toddler, I felt threat-
ened. I didn't want her in our box. I was scared and protective. I
had no room in my heart. But now, that mother, whomever she
will be, seems more real to me because of this poem. She will
give life, nationality, and the seed of talent; she will create the
child that I will raise as my own. She will be the most important
part of my new beginning. Because of the birth mother, I will
have the privilege of being a mother too.

––––––––

I place some adoption books from the library on my bedside
table as the phone rings. Eleanor Greenlee, my mentor in bioenergetic therapy, has called to console me on my baby losses.

She says, "I had my tubes tied, and I know how you feel."

Eleanor's words ring in my ears. I twirl the rubber phone
cord in my hand, unsure what to say back. She was my teacher

when I studied in San Francisco, but we haven't spoken in five years. It feels good to hear her voice.

I shrug. "Well, I don't know. It doesn't seem all that similar because you could have chosen to have them tied. Did you?"

She was silent for a second. "Actually, no. It was kind of complicated, and, well, how are you feeling right now? I mean, are you sure you want to hear my story?"

"Yes."

She continues. "I was seven months pregnant with a child we wanted. We were in for a routine ultrasound when I noticed concern on the radiologists' faces. They could not find a heartbeat."

I feel myself getting wobbly but I tell her to go on.

"The baby had died. I don't even know when. But the tough part was that, for two weeks, I had to carry a baby I knew was dead inside of me. And I kept hemorrhaging."

"Oh, my gosh. I'm so sorry. That must have been just horrible."

Her voice shakes, "Those two weeks were intolerable. I came very close to going crazy."

"So what happened?"

"The doctors made me deliver the dead baby without anesthesia. And they never let me see the baby. To be honest with you, going that low, feeling that out of control, is what led me to go to therapy for the first time."

I pull away from the phone to cushion this news. Close to crazy; carry a dead baby; deliver a dead baby; out of control. I can relate.

And she recovered and came back to live a vibrant life, one of international acclaim in her field.

When I get off the phone, what lingers in my mind is that this woman, whom I admire so much, had no relief from her intolerable misery, and her mind tried to protect her by coming close to splitting from reality. For some reason, it brings me comfort to know that any one of us can break, even the strongest ones. I wonder if hearing more people's survival stories might help me feel less alone during the times when my own grief blots out the sun.

————

In the phonebook, I find a self-help group for bereaved parents called The Empty Cradle. I ask Steve to attend a meeting, and he reluctantly agrees.

As we enter the big meeting room at the wellness clinic, I feel teary and cling to Steve's arm. Ellen, the wavy-haired leader in a flowery dress, approaches us, lays a hand on my shoulder, and smiles. I feel shy and unsure. We all sit in a circle as people introduce themselves and share bits of their stories, one at a time.

One woman says, "We decided we are finally going to take legal action against the Dalkon Shield. I am convinced it caused my infertility."

I sit up straight, suddenly very alert. Other couples nod like they know what she means. My eyes grow big, and I have to speak up. I lean forward. "I had the Dalkon Shield too. What are you all talking about?" One man answers, "There is a class action suit going on against the makers of the Dalkon Shield. They found direct evidence of the shield causing pelvic inflammatory disease, which causes infertility."

Though my doctor told me the Dalkon Shield may have caused my infertility, the idea of taking legal action is new. And here is a whole team of people, other victims like us, whose path we could follow.

One after another, the stories pour out: stillborn deaths, a neonatal death caused by doctor error, death of one twin and not the other, and a miscarriage at five months. The gravity of these losses hits the room like a sonic wave.

After some stories, I think, "Oh, that is worse than our story. I'm not sure I would have survived that. How did they get through it?"

Even the pouring out of the harshest loss, shot like an arrow from a bow, meets a cushion, as if the target is our group's circle of compassion that catches the story and lays it down gently. Here, we all gather in understanding and support. I feel a sense of belonging in this small room away from the world outside.

As one woman talks about her miscarriage, she sheds a few tears.

Her husband says, "I was only worried about her. I thought that men need to be strong and not feel, but then I burst into tears."

Steve squirms in his chair.

Joyce, who lost identical twins, says, "The world should stop for a day."

Everyone nods.

Her husband, Roger, puts his arm around his wife and says, "We will never be the same."

When it's our turn, I tell our story, my voice cracking, and then, I sob. I look around the room, sensing a warm space opening around me, and I inhale. I am sitting in a big bowl of love.

When the group session ends, I feel lighter as I walk with a spring in my step.

Steve is quiet as we climb into the car. As he drives, his eyes seem far away.

Trying to bring him back, I ask, "How did you like the meeting?"

He doesn't speak. Instead, he punches the brakes hard at a four-way stop. The sudden lurch of the car to a halt makes me grab the console and gasp.

He grips the wheel, drops his head, and sobs out loud. His cry bubbles up, and his tears drop onto his black shirt. As he calms, he says in a thin voice, "I was so focused on the dangers you faced in the hospital that I never grieved our babies."

I reach for him. We hold each other and cry.

———

Hearing about the Dalkon Shield lawsuit rattles my internal world. I am enraged, yet I notice that I also feel lighter, as if a rock of guilt has dislodged in my gut. My body didn't fail all on its own. Why did I trust those doctors so completely back then? I skim the phone book for the name of a lawyer who handles similar cases. With resolve, I dial her number, and by 10 a.m., I have joined the class action suit against the makers of the Dalkon Shield.

That night I wake up in a cold sweat from a bad dream.

Why did God allow this to happen to us? Even though the Dalkon Shield was at fault I wonder if I am being punished. My tight gut is a twisted tornado of anger as guilt and horror spin out of my control. As the tornado dies down, humility and powerlessness fill my whole body.

Sunday morning, I am lost in my own world. Steve pours me some tea. "You look far away. Are you okay?"

I shake my head. I am not okay. "I'm a little scared, Steve. This sadness feels different."

"What do you mean?"

"Well, for the last few nights, I have tried to pray, and no one was there. Nothing. I can't feel God's presence. I can't hear His voice. Waves of anxiety keep waking me up."

Steve sighs, and we lock eyes.

Steve and I go to church, where I hope to connect with God.

A young, dark-haired priest performs the solemn Mass. His sermon speaks right to me. "We need to have dependency on, and confidence in, Christ."

I tighten up and shake my head. No. My confidence has been deeply shaken.

Two days earlier, I was in the bathroom with cramps and feared they were a complication of surgery. On the toilet, I called out to God, afraid not to believe. Is that the best I, or any of us can do—believe out of fear? The bathroom cramps were temporary and gone by morning, but what lingers now is my distance from God.

I feel an uncomfortable hollowness inside my chest as the priest finishes his sermon.

Leaving the church, I look at the blue sky and say to myself—and to God— "I need help."

Chapter Twenty-Two

RIVER OF LOSS

I FLY NORTH and check myself into the Saint Francis Retreat House near my hometown to be alone for a week. The spiritual center is surrounded by a serene lake and acres of rolling hills. I plunk down my bag in a humble beige room and smile at this small holding cell that I hope can be a refuge.

I fall onto the twin bed and cry for a long time then pull out my journal and write:

I'm angry
and I'm sad
that I can never have my own baby,
that what I find beautiful in Steve
I can never reproduce in our own child.

I love Steve's handsome face, curious brain, and gentle manner. It would be exciting to see a little mini-Steve. I know we can love any child, no matter the genetics, but I am bluntly acknowledging all possible losses, and this is one.

I indulge in letting the river of loss fill my days. I trust this is what my body needs, so I let my body lead the way.

I spend most of the week crying alone on my bed and only

join clerics for meals and religious services. The world moves with me in slow motion and presents no demands. It becomes clear to me that the quiet pace of this place is meant for one thing. I am here to pour out buckets of tears to help wash away enough sorrow so I can make more room for love again, love for a new baby. I am adamant to do the work, so I can become ready to be a parent. I am not there yet. My vision is still clouded by grief.

I sit on the green grass near the mossy pond and watch a kingfisher dive down, searching for a fish, but like me, he comes up empty. I hike over the serene rolling hills of Hollister, slow and dumbfounded like the cows I pass. Calves are taken from their mothers as soon as they are born so the milk meant for the calf can be sold to humans. A brown cow chews grass. I look into her big, sad eyes. She has no power to be a mother. I am the kingfisher who can't catch a fish. I am the cow who can't keep her calf.

————

At the end of the week, my parents pick me up from the retreat house and drive to church for Mass on this Sunday night. My fragile soul has just begun peeking out, and I am hoping Mass will be soothing.

After communion, the priest says, "We have a special added ceremony tonight, the baptism of a new baby!"

His words freeze me. I hope I heard him wrong. I turn around to see a beaming young couple, dressed all in white, walking toward the front of the church, holding a baby in a long, white, linen pinafore, satin booties, and a white crocheted blanket.

As they pass our pew, my heart balloons with intense sorrow, and my eyes pool with tears that I cannot hold back. I stand up quickly, climb over my parents, and run out of the church. I enter the small bathroom and sob over the sink.

A few minutes later the door opens. In walks the mother of the baptized baby. She wears a long white gown that is backlit by a dim yellow bulb. She looks ethereal. I bow my head to hide my tears from her. Of all people, why does she show up? I choke back tears.

She looks at me as I wash my hands in the sink. "What's the matter?"

"I just lost a baby."

"I am so sorry. This must be so painful for you."

I look into her pink translucent face. Tears fill her blue-gray eyes as she places a gentle hand on my back. Warmth penetrates to my soul. She floats out the door and I look in the mirror, feeling healing light all around me. Humility and gratitude fill my heart and spread throughout my body. And then I smile. This was God sending me an earth angel. He is here.

———

Once I get back home, I feel a renewed connection with God and a washing away of so many tears that the thick fog of grief begins to dissipate. One morning I go through the motions of showering. As the hot water hits, I feel a sensation of contact, like the water pressure is tapping me on the shoulder and insisting I pay more attention.

I get dressed in my usual gray and khaki fog of indifference, drag a brush across my short hair, then shuffle to my jewelry box above my oak dresser. I open the box and look at all the earrings when a piece of amber catches my eye. Drawn to this fire-colored bauble, I pick up the earring, twirl it in my fingers, and admire its beauty. A warmth spreads in my chest. I have been walking in the dark for so long that this small pinpoint of light draws all my attention. So, caring what silly earrings to wear is to be my first spark of coming back to normal? This makes me giggle. I cross my fingers that my happier mood will prevail, because I am worried about being too depressed to have the energy for the adoption journey. I worry about having the wrong spirit, as that would not be fair to a child. I had to wait to feel better inside, and now I do. It has been weird to both have the longing to adopt yet feel the heavy chains of grief dragging me down. It feels like my shackles have been cut, and I can move forward without the loud clanking of those chains holding me back. This becomes another lesson for me to learn, that the timing of my moods, of the world's readiness, and of God's plans are not up to me. I humbly pray these chains are gone for good.

The next day, I awake with the same happy spark and the next as well, and slowly the gray skies fade, and sunshine penetrates my skin every day. I am no longer gripped by sorrow. I feel so relieved to kick off the slippers of depression so I can pour my whole heart into adoption.

I say to Steve, "I think I am going to start calling adoption lawyers again."

Chapter Twenty-Three

ADOPTION TRAIL

Private

I SPEND three hours on the phone. Each lawyer sounds confident and upbeat. I am surprised at how fast the process might unfold, but I am also confused by how it all works.

The third lawyer does his best to explain the landscape of adoption.

"There are generally four routes adoptive parents can take. The first might be where a family member or someone you know is pregnant and they want to give you their baby."

"How often does that happen?"

"Not very often. The second is that you contact a lawyer like me who is also in contact with birth parents seeking good adoptive parents."

"So you have birth parents who contact you directly?"

"Yes. Let me tell you the other two options. The third route is to go through a private agency, like Catholic Charities. This can be difficult for parents because you have to go through excessive screening. The fourth option is going through a county agency, which almost no one likes because it takes forever. International adoptions have a lot of legal requirements and travel costs."

"What do you recommend?"

"Generally, adoptive parents find using a private lawyer to be the fastest route with the least amount of hassle."

I thank him and feel I understand the process a little better.

On my next call, a self-assured lawyer says, "You know, I may have a promising lead on a baby for you to adopt."

I hold the phone in the air. After all my physical pain and heartache, I make this one phone call, and there might be a baby ready for adoption? Right now?

The lawyer provides a few details, says he needs to make some calls and that he will be getting in touch with me the next day to offer the specifics.

My spirit rides high into the sky. I hang up the phone thinking this lawyer is my fairy godmother. My mind races. Can it really be this easy?

Do I call Steve now? How much work would it take to get the nursery up and running? We don't have anything ready, and I had planned to paint a mural on the nursery wall. When Steve gets home, I give him a big hug and share the news.

"The lawyer I just talked to has a promising lead on a baby. He will call when he knows more."

Steve says, "Well, wait a minute. I mean this seems kind of fast. What do we really know about all this? I want to be supportive though."

I am up as far as the seesaw will take me, and I haven't felt this much hope in a while, but here is Steve, bringing me down with his need for information and caution. The top of the seesaw is happiness and energy and hope, but I see that it can mean staring at the clouds without my feet on the ground. So, it isn't a place to stay forever. I know I need to come back down to earth, not so I lose hope and get depressed but to face the challenges on this new path. But I find that so hard, when I want what I want so badly.

The next day the phone rings. I rush to pick it up.

"Yes?"

The lawyer is apologetic. "I'm so sorry, but this baby won't work out. The birth mother changed her mind and wants to keep her baby."

My heart sinks. There it is. Negativity. Another possibility is gone like sand through my fingers. I am so myopic in my fever to adopt that I don't think about the other side much at all. Maybe that baby is better off with her birth mother, but I can only see my own dreams right now.

I take a breath, stand up and dust myself off after tumbling down. I am undeterred and start marching back up the hill. If that lawyer has leads, then other lawyers might have them as well. I pick up my yellow pages and call the next lawyer listed.

He too is confident. "Oh, yes, we are always receiving calls from birth moms who are looking for quality adoptive parents. We are one of the biggest representing firms in town, and we are always in need of couples just like you."

I get that the term "couples just like you" is mentioned to flatter me when he knows nothing about me, and it dawns on me that these lawyers are in the business of making money from adoptive parents.

"Is it a difficult process?"

"Oh, no. There is a little bit of paperwork, but it's not too bad at all. We simply make an introduction, and if you are chosen by the birth parents, arrangements are made, and that's all there is to it." He makes it sound simple. Too simple. My guess is that not much screening goes on. But I am in the thrall of rushing forward, which loves to bypass my sensible brain.

"So, how soon could this happen?"

"I actually have to return a call I just received this morning from the parents of a pregnant teenager. She's due in three months. The girl is very young, and they say there is no way she can take care of it. They want a better life for their grandchild. So if all goes well, it might just be the perfect match for you."

I can almost hear the baby-train whistle coming to town. Only three months from now. How exciting. I imagine having a small baby during wintertime and bundling them up in a cozy jacket with a hood adorned with panda bear ears. I think of growing up with eight younger brothers and sisters and all the time I spent playing with them and helping them. When I was ten, I carried my baby brother, Peter, on my hip that whole summer. His smile lit up the house. That was true every time a new baby came home. Being with younger ones is in my blood.

"Can I take your number, and I will let you know when I hear more? I promise to call as soon as I know something. It shouldn't be too long."

For the next few days, I go to work, exercise, come home, and make dinner, but I can't stop thinking about having a new baby in just three short months. Every time I pass the phone I will it to ring with good news from the lawyer. Why hasn't he called? He said it wouldn't be that long. What is going on over there? After two more days, my fingers are itching to call him, but I was told to wait.

Ten days later, the lawyer finally calls. "The grandparents decided they would raise the baby. I'm sorry."

Grandparents are probably a good idea, and I'm happy they get to keep their family together, but my wishful heart that chose winter clothes for this baby I now can't raise sinks to the floor. I thank the lawyer robotically. I hang up the phone.

I can't believe that, just like that, another one falls through. I am beginning to understand that none of this is going to be quick or easy. My longing makes me move so fast that I stay naïve and don't question motives; I am afraid to pause long enough to consider what is best for others, like birth families; or to think about the motives of greedy lawyers. Why do I do that? I think my speediness protects me from feeling too much disappointment. And disappointment can plunge me into depression. So I set my jaw and try and outrun anything that tries to stop my dream.

I am stunned for a day but bounce back, determined to keep searching. I call an adoption agency listed in the yellow pages. As I ask questions, I learn this isn't a public agency, as advertised, but an agency aligned with a ministry and run by volunteers.

The woman on the phone asks me a series of probing questions: "Are you born-again? Are you in Renew? Are you in Bible study?"

Her questions make me nervous. *Uh-oh. They want someone who fits an exact religious profile.* I feel uncomfortable being pressed about my religious views, but I tell myself to stay open.

"I am in a Bible study group in my parish, but I am also a feminist."

She sounds offended. "Well, you know, of course, that men are the head of the household!"

Her rigid view and high, pinched voice make me feel boxed in. It isn't a match.

As I hang up the phone I think about the pro-life, pro-choice debate and my mother, who was a faithful Catholic. As a young woman her parents needed her income from her job as a grocery store clerk to help them feed their family. She was so devout that she would never work on Sundays. She told her boss, "If you make me work on Sunday, I will quit."

When she was in her sixties, my mother helped found a program called the "The Crisis Pregnancy Center." It was a Christian organization that counseled pregnant teens, provided free screenings, and encouraged adoption as an alternative to abortion.

She worked there for ten years, and when I was in my thirties, my mother took me on a tour. The crisis center was housed in an old, white, wooden Victorian home. As we walked the halls we peered into a room with a sonogram machine. My mom shared with me that many women came to the center only to use the free sonogram machine to confirm that they were pregnant. Then, they wanted to leave and get an abortion.

My mother was pro-life, and this bothered her. But the women and girls were required to do one counseling session. She had one chance to help change their minds and counsel them toward the path of adoption.

We walked into her small office, which held a desk and a chair. "So many girls and women sit across from me at this desk and cry," my mother said. "Some have children they can't afford, some have serious health complications, some are very young and are not ready to be mothers, and some are in abusive marriages." Her eyes looked faraway. "There are all kinds of reasons that they can't give birth." She sounded weighed down and touched by their pain. Then her eyes focused, and she looked straight at me. "My Catholic faith promotes a pro-life stance, and I am personally against abortion, but after counseling so many desperate young women, my heart has shifted, and I have become pro-choice." Hitting her flattened palm on her heavy wooden desk, she said, "This life-changing decision should be up to the woman and not controlled by the church or the state."

I had never expected to hear that sentence coming out of my mother's mouth. I felt moved by her thoughtfulness. Her ability to shift her perspective impressed me and touched my heart.

———

I remain grateful for my mother's strong character and her ability to progress toward a view that chooses to honor a woman's sovereignty over her body.

The next day, I put in a call to Catholic Charities Adoption Services. The social worker, Pam, is open and informative. I feel relieved that she does not sound religiously dogmatic like the born-again fundamentalist I talked to yesterday.

Pam says, "We are not rigid about religious affiliation, just looking for solid, loving couples."

After I share our history, she notes, "Actually, you fit the criteria of what we are looking for as an ethnic 'blend' because you are half Spanish."

I perk up. "Oh, that's good to hear."

"Most girls want parents who are some ethnic mix and also Catholic. But it varies, so we want a broad selection for them to choose from. Girls get to pick the adoptive parents."

I like that the girls get to choose because I have heard that parents or other adults often dictate and the girls have no say.

Pam says the birth parents enter counseling with Sister Barbara, who directs the program. She counsels them once a month throughout the whole process.

I nod, acknowledging that the birth parents are given space to process this life-changing decision. But it isn't just the birth parents who get counseling. Pam says, "Each adoptive couple joins other couples in an eight-week group course on under-standing all the dynamics and procedures of adoption."

I like this kind of holding environment that respects all parties. I am eager to learn more.

"That seems very thorough. How do you charge?"

"Well, we have a sliding scale and charge eight percent of your gross income."

I sigh, thinking that is fairer than the high flat fee the lawyers charge.

As we close our conversation, Pam suggests I read the book, *Beating the Adoption Game,* by a local author named Cynthia D. Martin. She says the book will orient me and give me useful background on the whole process.

I am not certain, yet, that we will choose Catholic Charities as our agency, but as soon as I get off the phone with Pam, I call Ms. Martin directly to see if she has advice on local resources.

When her assistant JoAnn answers, I say, "I'm seeking adop-tion services, and Ms. Martin's book was recommended by Pam, the social worker at Catholic Charities."

"Oh, you are? Well, *I* am giving up *my* child for adoption."

This knocks me sideways. What did she just say? Could this

be true? I take a breath to center myself, but excitement takes over. Could my search end right here through this random connection? I try to act calm, as if I have talked directly to a birth mother before.

"Ah, what kind of family are you looking for?"

Her voice is sturdy. "Well, I want someone to care for and love the child, and one parent should have dark hair. I am Caucasian; my boyfriend is half Mexican. The baby is due in October or November."

I share with her that we fit that description as my husband is Caucasian and I am half Spanish.

She says, "This could work. Let me give you some details."

My heart races with so much hope that I have to concentrate on her every word in order to stay focused. My hand quivers as I grab a pen and notepad.

She tells me to call her OB-GYN so we can coordinate with him about the birth plan and adds, "I'll inform him that you'll be calling." She explains that she will pay for the birth on her own and that her parents want her to move. After she mumbles something about being a surrogate that I don't understand, I thank her and promise to follow through.

I hang up the phone, and my spirits soar on wings of hope. I am back doing what I do: naïvely flying so fast I can't slow enough to consider any problems.

The next day, I call her doctor and gush confidently about how we would like to coordinate with their birth plan in adopting JoAnn's baby.

The doctor is adamant. "I was not contacted by her and do not have a patient by that name."

What? Was this whole thing some joke? Shock holds my chest frozen on the inhale, and my heart starts to get wobbly. He's never heard of her? I feel pushed away by this sudden turn of events and by the doctor's impatience, so I thank him and hang up the phone.

My mind flutters like a drunken butterfly. What is going on?

Is she crazy? Was she making it up? Why would she send me to a doctor?

A sense of betrayal overcomes me. I feel like a kite in a capricious wind, on a quick high, then dropped just as quickly as the wind dies. This receptionist of Ms. Martin makes me too wary to pursue the adoption book.

A month later, after two more leads from lawyers fall through, I plop on my bed, exhausted. Steve walks in, notices my eyes filling with tears, and scoops me up in a bear hug. His warmth softens my tense chest.

I confess, "These leads keep falling through, and it's killing me. How many babies do we have to lose before we get to keep one?"

He takes a long, slow breath. "I think you're suffering too much with this. Let's not take the private route anymore. No more lawyers or random people promising you babies. You keep getting excited then heartbroken. I think, from now on, we should only go to county or city agencies."

A part of me is still clinging onto the fast fix, the promised "quick and easy" route, but I know he is right. I have been knocked to the ground too many times. It's time to stop looking up to the sky for a stork to drop me a baby.

Chapter Twenty-Four
ADOPTION TRAIL

Agencies

THE HANDMADE SIGN on the door reads, "County Adoptions Orientation."

We enter the large, plain auditorium to join a hundred others who take their seats in metal folding chairs. As I sit, I hope I am finally in the right room. I look at the faces, imagining them to be like us: people who can't have a baby, people who have been down the same road of infertility, medical interventions, disappointments, and loss. I feel a kind of camaraderie as well as urgency in the room. We are all here to move on, to take decisive action. To start our families.

A stocky, brown-haired, middle-aged woman in glasses stands at the podium, shifting from one foot to the other, impatient for us to settle so she can get started.

The room quiets, and she begins. "You all are here thinking you can adopt a newborn, right?"

She tips her chin down and peers at all of us over her reading glasses like an impatient teacher.

We are hungry birds in a nest, eager for a worm from mother.

"Well, guess what? There aren't many newborns up for adoption."

She sucks all the air out of the room. I look around, noticing others feeling what I feel, deflated. She continues, and years of irritation linger in her voice.

"Look, here's the honest truth. San Diego has a backlog of older children who really need good homes. They're stuck in temporary placements, and all they want is a forever home. Please consider adopting an older child."

I squirm and immediately think of potential problems with children who are older. They have already had parents who were unreliable, which is likely to make them less trusting.

Unwavering, she goes on. "These kids in foster care need good homes. You can also do 'fost-adopt.' That's where you have them in your home temporarily as a trial and then consider adoption."

No one nods. No one smiles.

"Foster children are available much sooner than newborns."

Undeterred, a man raises his hand and asks what we all want to know: "What is the wait time for a newborn?"

She sighs. To her, we are another one-track-mind group she is unlikely to sway. "For a baby under the age of one, the wait is between two and five years."

She keeps talking, but I don't hear much after that.

The meeting ends. A few people still have an eager look in their eyes, and they approach the speaker.

As I stand, fold my chair, and place against the wall, I know this place does not hold the answer we are seeking.

On the car ride home, I say to Steve, "Two-to-five years feels way too long."

Hands on the steering wheel, eyes forward, he nods in agreement.

I pull out my sketchpad and draw a giant sperm rising like a hot air balloon. I write, "Steve's sperm" on it. I draw a syringe next to it, labeled, "Artificial insemination." I then draw tiny images of Steve and me standing together way behind a pregnant woman. Her maternity top says, "Surrogate."

As Steve pulls the car into the carport and turns off the engine, I show him my sketch, and he says, "No. I do not want to do that at all."

I ask, "Why not?"

He shakes his head. "I want a child to be from both our bodies, or neither."

I respect that.

I spend the next hour thinking about in vitro because that would be an answer that involves both of us. Sitting at the kitchen table, I draw all the procedures for in vitro fertilization, such as me popping Pergonal, extra eggs emerging from the ovary, doctors retrieving the eggs in surgery, eggs being fertilized in a petri dish, and the doctor placing the eggs in my uterus.

I draw a big picture of my face in my hands, a face in waiting. At the bottom of the page, I write:

No implantation = no baby +$7,000. Per cycle. For failure.

The cost of trying.

Or . . . implantation!

And we will get what we've wanted for so long. No price is too high to make our dream come true.

I show Steve, and he says, "We can't afford those fees."

I know this, but it still hurts.

I look at my drawing of the syringe and the sperm one more time. The idea of walking into another hospital makes me cringe, so the idea of in vitro fertilization fades away. I close my sketchbook. I just have to let myself play one last time with options that might take less than "two to five years" wait, as we just learned from the county adoption meeting.

I wake up the next morning, fully focused back on adoption. I pull out my sketchpad to draw "The Adoption Option."

I write in blue marker, "What is your range of acceptance?"

When calling about adoption, one person had asked me this question. I was surprised and said, "Ah, I don't know." It was a weird question, and kind of cold-hearted, as if we were discarding all the bruised and uneven apples in search of "the perfect one." I draw seven children of different colors and with varied abilities. And I give them all bright eyes and big smiles.

A week later, we go to an adoption orientation meeting at a state agency. This one is similar to the first but without the guilt-and-shame-inducing tone directed at those who hope to adopt newborns. But they agreed with the county agency that "It will take at least two years to adopt an infant locally."

Our third stop is a Catholic Charities orientation. This is the agency where I spoke with Pam by phone, and she seemed kind and thoughtful. At the Catholic Charities orientation, Sister Barbara, a warm, round-faced woman, welcomes each person as they arrive. She shows us to our seats then gives an introduction about the adoption program.

My ears perk up when she mentions that "most adoptions take about one year."

The shorter timeline is encouraging.

Her eyes sparkle and I like her right away. She is a kind-hearted soul, committed to both the birth parents and the adoptive couple. She shares how the process works. She counsels the birth parents weekly in the months before their child is born. She leads an eight-week ongoing support group for prospective adoptive couples, and a licensed social worker comes to the group to speak about the legal protocol and protections involved in adoption.

It all sounds good to me, but we know I jump into things. And maybe I feel at home because I am Catholic. Should I trust that?

Steve is the cautious, often more sensible one, so I need to check with him.

I look at Steve with anxious hope. "What do you think?"

He says, "I like them. They seem to care, and I like that the legal and financial steps are clear."

I exhale in relief. After the orientation, Steve and I walk up to Sister Barbara's desk, and my heart pumps with hope-filled promise as we sign up for the next adoption parenting class.

Chapter Twenty-Five

RELINQUISH

IN OUR FIRST EVENING CLASS, we sit in a circle with five other couples, all eagerly waiting for Sister Barbara to arrive. These are couples who have been on a similar journey through child loss and, like us, are eager to adopt. I smile at them in solidarity.

Scanning the room, I see one red-haired, middle-aged man wearing a plaid shirt and a huge wooden crucifix around his neck. How Catholic do we need to be here? Or is he trying to impress Sister Barbara? Will that work? Will it matter?

Sister Barbara walks in, offers us cookies and tea, and asks us to go around the room and introduce ourselves to each other. One couple shares that their baby died shortly after birth, and after that, the wife was unable to conceive. Another couple shares that, after five miscarriages, they were told the mother was unable to carry a baby to term. A third couple shares that, after a year of trying and endless testing, the husband was told he had unviable or "lazy" sperm, that his sperm would never make it to the egg.

As each story is shared, the room changes. My self-consciousness fades. I no longer worry about how I look, what I'm wearing, and whether a crucifix around one's neck matters.

As each couple reveals their heartbreak, I feel a common space open up. We have traveled similar roads, experienced hopelessness and loss, and now we find ourselves here in this room. It is like we came out of the woods scratched and bloody, met as strangers at a new opening, and can now travel the next road together.

Over the weeks, our cohort of six couples builds a new circle of friendship.

But during the fourth week of training to become adoptive parents, I tap my foot impatiently, tired of listening again as the social worker talks about the details of legal issues we will experience in the adoption game. I smile attentively, but my mind floats off as I think, "Yeah, yeah, yeah. I just want a baby."

Sister Barbara stands and walks in front of us to a huge screen the size of a wall. She clicks it on and looks at us. We stare at a giant photo of a teenaged birth mother who is leaning over a piece of paper. She is crying while signing a form to relinquish all of her parental rights.

I freeze.

I stare at the girl on the screen. I want to escape out the window and fly away from here, and hold onto my own delusions that this is just about me and what I want. I do not want to care about her, but I can't take my eyes off of her. Her head leaning over the form. Her long brown hair falling over her bare shoulders. Her tears. Her tense hand holding the pen. Signing away her rights to her child. My eyes betray me and fill with tears. My heart is captured. I stay put and do not fly away.

As Sister Barbara describes this new landscape, my whole being fills with care and concern for the birth parents and the pain they must face in making what must be the most difficult decision of their lives. One that will follow them forever.

I soak up Sister Barbara's description of the "adoption triangle," a term for the relationship and dynamics among the baby, the birth parents, and the adoptive parents.

She notes, "You need to have compassion and think about

what is best for all parties, not just what is best for you as adoptive parents." She has been around and must know we need this lesson. She must know how self-absorbed we've been as we focus on our very important goal.

"We work with the birth parents to create the best plan, which we feel is open adoption. Open adoption is where the biological parents participate in the experience of placing their child with an adoptive family. It also means that they may choose to continue to have contact with you as the adoptive parents. Open placement is a further step that happens sometimes, where the birth parents hand you the baby in person."

I squirm in my seat. Do I want that experience?

She continues, "We suggest that you send photos of the baby once a month for the first year and then one each year after that. Both birth parents must sign away all legal rights to parent their child. After that moment, they have twenty-four hours to change their minds."

I am thinking that the twenty-four-hour window is respectful, giving them time to reconsider and avoid being impulsive. It must be a torturous decision. Those twenty-four hours must be dizzying for the birth family.

Sister Barbara says, "If they do not call us within that twenty-four-hour window, then we call you, the adoptive parents. That's the moment when I get to say, 'You have a new baby.'"

Hearing those words makes everyone in the circle light up.

Leaving us with that last line, "You have a new baby," Sister Barbara smiles. I can tell she loves all three parts of the triangle—helping babies find loving homes, respectfully counseling the birth parents, and making dreams come true for adoptive couples.

"This concludes your eight-week course." Sister Barbara stands up, looks at us warmly, gathers her papers, and is ready to usher us out of her office.

But none of us move. I look around at the other couples,

feeling a sense of connection in my bones. We don't want to leave each other.

Mary says, "We have to keep in touch. I want to know what happens with each of you."

Everyone nods.

Steve says, "That would be great. We can support each other through the year of waiting."

I exhale, feeling both excitement and fear. I see the same mix of feelings in the eyes of the other men and women. We exchange numbers and give warm hugs. We still need to hold each other's hands—and now we are all ready for the ride.

Chapter Twenty-Six

BUILDING A NEST

THIS RIDE IS FOCUSED on waiting for our adopted baby. Every time I see a mother pushing a baby stroller, my eyes follow with jealousy and hope. Patience has never been my strong suit, but I am learning that there is nothing I can do to rush the process. I am grateful for my work—that I have something else to do other than wait. Being able to help someone else gives me meaning. I am no longer struggling with depression and indifference, like when I had to return to work too soon after my ectopic surgeries. I find it easier to empathize with my clients and their own pain.

On many weekends, I teach as part of the local faculty of the bioenergetics training program. I love bioenergetics because it works with the body as well as the mind, but I notice that it isn't a fit for some of my new clients.

I look around and dip my toe into another emerging psychotherapy model: self-psychology. My colleague, Bob, says, "Read Heinz Kohut. Everyone is buzzing about needing ways to work with very fragile clients, and Kohut has great ideas. Check it out." Bob lends me Kohut's *The Analysis of the Self*, where the focus is on the stance of the therapist as a healing force that can help fill the holes in a person's psyche. I am excited to learn this new method, dive in further, and read related books. I join a self-psychology supervision group connected to the psychoanalytic community and am stimulated by the case discussions. I find myself innovating and creating new tools, combining my work in bioenergetics with self-psychology.

I write and publish a paper explaining how the two methods work well together to enhance therapy.

One day I get a call from a colleague who asks, "Can you lead a one-day training on bioenergetics and self-psychology at our annual retreat? Our students read your paper in the journal, and they can't wait to hear more."

I am thrilled to be recognized in this new way, especially because I can't control any aspect of the adoption waiting game. I can only wait. The clock is the boss. I look at the clock and say to myself, "Dear Lord, grant me the patience to accept what I cannot change."

"I would love to!" I exclaim. I get off the phone and squeal like a child invited to Disneyland. It is my first invitation to lead a training that I get to design by myself.

My morning lecture goes well, but I feel more vulnerable in the afternoon, where I intend to ask for a volunteer to help me demonstrate the two methods. I have never done a demonstration in a course before. What if it doesn't work?

After lunch, I take a walk among the majestic pines and breathe in the warm air. I tell myself to just be in the moment and let it unfold. I need courage to do my first demonstration in front of a group, so I pray, "Lord, help me find the courage to take on this scary task."

When the class resumes, I stand in the middle of the half circle and ask, "Does anyone want to volunteer to do a session?"

Silence. The men in the room look surprised and tense up.

I can hear the sound of the clock ticking. I fake confidence by puffing up my chest, but my smile is strained as the silence lingers forever.

Finally, a woman volunteers, and I want to hug her for taking a chance on me.

She walks toward me, and I smile at her. I soon forget the audience and focus only on her and myself. We create a bubble in the middle of a circle. I breathe and follow her breath. I am fully present. She shares her emotional pain openly, and what unfolds is a session that beautifully combines the two modalities.

I picture myself falling back onto a couch with a big smile. From that moment on, by having the courage to do it this first time, I know I will be able to perform good sessions in front of any crowd, anywhere, anytime. I changed something I could change—my willingness to take a chance on myself. I did a session in front of others that could have failed. But I did it anyway, and it was a success.

That night I join an outdoor sing-along around a campfire at the woodsy retreat center on campus. I look at my colleagues, and in the glow of this magical night, my body and spirit expand to fullness.

When I get home the first call I receive is from Carol, who is a woman in our couples adoption group. We have all been staring down time for eight months while waiting for babies.

"Guess what?"

"What?"

"Sister Barbara called us two days ago. We picked up our new baby boy yesterday. He is so beautiful. He is the sweetest little thing. We are so in love!"

"Oh, Carol, I am so happy for you. What's his name?"

"Andy. We are already calling him Andy Pandy."

I congratulate Carol and promise we will make it to their baby welcoming party the next week for Andy. Andy Pandy.

I get off the phone and sigh. My body comes to life in a new way. The heat of hope flows through my torso. I look down at my arms and turn them up and down. These arms could soon be holding a new baby. We are entering a new land. I run over to

Steve and give him a hug. Now we know the dream is possible. Will we be next in line?

———

I stand in the nursery, hand painting very small bouquets of red, yellow, and blue balloons in row after row on the wall. Meditative and a great way to calm my nerves, it makes me feel serene, even unrushed, which is rare for me.

Once the two walls are painted, I make a large mural of a clown holding balloons on the wall above the new diaper-changing table. I hang sweet white lace curtains and place a white wooden crib in the room. Perfect for a new girl or boy. I am a bird picking out twigs and flying them through the air to build a new nest. I whistle, and it reminds me of my mother whistling as she folded clothes when she was pregnant.

Steve walks in and smiles, charmed by the vibrant colors that dance on the walls. I follow his eyes; he looks around as if imagining the new life that will soon fill this space. He kisses me on the cheek and hums as he walks out of the room.

———

Now, we have been waiting ten months, and that promised one-year mark will approach quickly. I imagine I hear a distant drumbeat whenever I look at the phone. Will that beat get closer and louder soon? I sense our call is imminent.

I want to stay connected to the adoption community, so I attend a local seminar where both an adoptive mother and a birth mother speak about their experiences. I greet others from our Catholic Charities adoption group who are also in attendance.

At the break, I learn that another couple in our cohort, Jesse and Janis, have just gotten their baby. I am happy for them, but I smile stiffly to hide my usual impatience.

I look up to see Sister Barbara coming straight toward me. Her eyes twinkle as she leans in and says, "So good to see you."

She pulls back, hesitates, then leans toward me again, this time close to my face. She whispers, "Your ears must be burning. Call us if you go on vacation."

She wouldn't mention vacation unless she had a baby almost ready for us. I freeze in anticipation but can't ask her for any more information because of the rules. We are not supposed to be involved with the process at all until twenty-four hours after the birth parents have signed away their parental rights.

After the seminar, I float home. I know that Sister Barbara was trying to tell me we might be getting a baby soon. Even though she wasn't supposed to.

Chapter Twenty~Seven

LICHEN

July 1986, Utah

MY ENTIRE WORLD revolves around the phone. I am a hawk flying in slow circles above it.

Three long weeks pass, and it is hard to concentrate. While at work, I worry I will miss the call at home from Sister Barbara. When I am home, I jump every time the phone rings.

On Monday, I call Catholic Charities to tell them our summer vacation plans.

The following night, there is a voice message from Sister Barbara. It is a cryptic, "Please call. Don't get excited."

I don't know what that means. I call back immediately and am told she is gone for the day.

I call early the following morning and speak to Debra, the assistant, who shares that Sister Barbara will not be in until noon.

"Do you know what this is about?" I ask.

"Sorry, I don't know."

I hang up the phone with a nervous feeling in my gut. I try to distract myself with toast and a book. Time slows, but my thoughts race. What could have happened? She seemed so positive at the seminar, telling me to alert her about when we are going on vacation. But that was three weeks ago. So much can happen in three weeks.

Just after noon, the phone rings. I spring to pick it up.

Sister Barbara's voice is soft and low, almost apologetic. "The placement fell through." I sink into the couch and hold my forehead in my hand while she explains. "What happened was that one of our birth parent couples, Tim and Megan, had picked you as adoptive parents before they had the baby. Then, six weeks ago, she had the baby. When I saw you at the seminar, I thought it was a sure thing. But after placing the baby in foster care, Megan showed up and took the baby home. She couldn't decide. She kept changing her mind. Her only focus seemed to be holding onto Tim. She wanted to keep the baby so that Tim would stay. Then, she wanted to give up the baby so that Tim would stay. And then when you called with your vacation schedule yesterday, I thought it only fair to tell you they have decided against adoption." She ends by saying, "You'd be much better parents for this baby—but I guess it wasn't meant to be."

I cry off and on for the next two hours. This young birth mother seems only interested in Tim and not the welfare of her baby. I worry about the baby and hope the mother learns to focus on loving her child.

It does help that Sister Barbara said we would be better parents.

It all swims in my head, and I lie back on my pillow and tell God, "This year has been long, and I am weary."

I hear His guidance in my head. "I know. You have been through a lot."

I nod. "You never said I would get things my way."

"That is right."

I wonder aloud, "But am I ever going to get a baby?"

"What did I say?"

I sit up, more alert now. "You said, 'And everything else you will receive.'"

My mind goes back to my spiritual retreat in Big Sur, before I met Steve. How surprised and humbled I was to hear God respond to my angst when I was lost and reached toward Him from a desperate need. And it is the words "you will receive" that bring me back to God time and time again when I forget or doubt Him. They remind me that He is real.

Sometimes, I have to shuffle too long in frustration through a junky drawer full of papers and clips and hair ties to remember again that, indeed, the amber jewel is in the drawer. The jewel that is God. Then, I hold the jewel and remember again: He spoke to me. He walked with me through my baby losses, and He walks with me on this quest toward motherhood.

Now, God tells me, "Then keep the flame alive. Stay humble. Trust in My goodness."

———

We head to Utah for summer vacation as planned. I stand, looking at the vast, striped Rocky Mountains in Zion National Park. A river flows to our left. It is a warm day in July.

As we hike down the soft red sand, Steve pauses to lean over a moss-covered boulder on the side of the road. "Ooh, look at this. Lichens are spreading on this rock!"

All I see are two different greenish globs hugging the rock.

He points. "This one is lichen, and this one is moss. The moss is a plant. The moss and lichen are competing for space."

"What is lichen?"

"It is a fungus with a symbiotic alga inside it."

I shrug my shoulders, unsure of what he is talking about—but it's fun to see the enthusiasm in his eyes.

"I wonder how long this has been here," he says. "Or how much a lichen travels in a year across the rock." His eyes widen.

"Oh, I know. Let's measure it, come back next year, and see how far it moves."

How much a lichen travels in a year? He wants to come back next year and see how far slow-moving lichen travels in a year? Like how many tenths of an inch? Steve has always been more patient. Steve can cling to the rock and keep moving forward, albeit slowly.

I think about our travels across the rock of life in the past year—from two ectopic pregnancies to the ups and downs of the adoption journey.

I take in the landscape and feel some comfort. This is the same place we honeymooned three years earlier and dreamed of starting a family.

A family with seven children hikes near us. The parents look as happy as my parents looked when they took us on excursions. The park is filled with large, happy families.

I don't have that old jealousy that used to overwhelm me when my loss and longing felt more raw.

A father walks the red dirt path, holding the hand of his young son, and I think of Steve as a father-to-be. At the visitors station earlier, Steve picked up a junior ranger application, looked it over, and placed it in his pack. "This is for when our child comes with us to Zion."

I can't help but smile at this image of us walking with a toddler through this glorious park.

Chapter Twenty-Eight

THE CALL

One Month Later, August 1986

I GRAB my tennis racket and call down the hallway to my sister, Bonny. "Are you dressed?"

She walks into the room in her tennis whites, racket in hand. "Let's go, Susy!" It's the nickname my family has called me since I was a little girl.

Bonny has been visiting us for a week, and we are preparing to drive to our annual family doubles tennis tournament in Hollister. It is a long drive from San Diego, but if we leave in the next twenty minutes, we will make it on time for the first match.

I pluck my tennis shoes from the closet then twirl my racket. "We are going to take home the trophy this year. You just wait and see." I lace up one shoe and raise the other foot onto the bed when the phone rings. My watch reads 3 p.m.

"This is Sister Barbara from Catholic Charities."

I sit on my bed in slow motion. My heart skips a beat. "Yes, ah, hello, Sister."

"Congratulations. You have a new baby girl." Her voice is buoyant.

I clutch the phone, unsure what I have just heard. "Ah, no, uh, we are on our way to a family tennis tournament."

"I think this is more important." She chuckles.

I wave my arms to get my sister's attention. I take a breath. "Yes, Sister. So sorry. I'm just shocked."

"No worries. This happens all the time. You will pick up your baby at 3 p.m. tomorrow in the same room where you went to the adoption classes. I will be there with your social worker. The foster mother and birth parents will also be there."

My head swirls in a twirl of emotions. This is it. It's happening. It's real. I want to jump up and run down the street, screaming in joy, but I also want to sit still and ask a million questions.

"You will get all the relevant details tomorrow. Oh, and don't forget to bring diapers and a baby car seat." She pauses then adds, "You'll be okay. See you tomorrow."

I don't know if I say goodbye. Maybe I say, "Okay, thanks." That seems so meager. I'm frozen with a phone in my ear, a little outside of myself, having flown through the galaxy to a new universe. Diapers? Car seat? Real, actual things for a real, actual can-it-be-true baby. A baby for us? For us!

My sister and Steve stand wide-eyed in the doorway of my bedroom. They stare at me like two meerkats at attention. How long have they been standing here? I come back to this planet, my house, and this bedroom, and my voice breaks as I say, "We have a baby girl!"

Steve looks stunned and jumps forward in two giant steps to hug me.

"We pick her up at 3 p.m. tomorrow."

He scans the room wildly. "What do we need to do to be ready in twenty-four hours?"

I jump up, and together, as if on a trampoline of exhilaration, we hop about. "We already have a bag. We need to pack it with baby stuff. Where is that bag?"

Bonny watches us act like two chickens with our heads cut off and takes a sensible step. "You want me to call Mom and Dad?"

Bonny loves sharing family news, and I give her the honor. She rings them in Hollister. "Dad, is Mom there with you? She needs to hear this too."

I overhear Dad yell out, "Ramona, get in here!"

Bonny looks at me as she sits on my bed with the phone to her ear. She winks at me as she tells our parents, "Susy and Steve just got the call. They have a new baby girl and will pick her up tomorrow."

I hear them say, "Awww . . ." as Bonny puts the phone to my ear.

Dad says, "We have been waiting for this good news and praying it would happen. Every new baby is a blessing."

Mom's voice chokes up. "Oh, Susy, we are so happy for you."

My heart catches in my throat, and tears fill my eyes. Mom is not the gushing type, so this surprises me, and I linger here. I take a breath and inhale fully. This moment between me and my mother feels especially sacred, as if I hold an empty cup, reaching toward her with tentative arms, and she is turning toward me to fill that cup with her love. "Thank you. I can't believe it. I'm so happy."

I hang up the phone, stand up and squeeze Steve long and hard. Our joint euphoria makes us float to the ceiling like helium balloons finally set free.

Bonny joins us in our excitement.

We all shout, "Woohoo!" and raise our fists over and over.

I hover, elated, dancing on clouds of anticipatory baby-love all night long. Visions of sugarplums dance in my head because the doors to a baby were closed, and now, they are open.

Having loved my younger brothers and sisters, I didn't have a preference for a boy or girl. But now we are having a girl, and I am ready to go. I can't wait to walk through the door of the OshKosh B'gosh store to pick out cute denim overalls, cotton lace cut-out blouses, and sweet little dresses and booties. I see myself combing her hair and attaching ribbons and barrettes. She can be any kind of girl she wants to be—brainy, artistic, boyish, athletic, girly—and I will champion her dreams and love her to death.

Chapter Twenty~Nine
OPEN PLACEMENT

AFTER A RESTLESS NIGHT of anxious anticipation, I sit up, smiling ear to ear. I go to the closet and put on a pink cotton summer dress (I never wear pink, but it's a girl!) and a pearl necklace.

Buckling in the car seat is surreal and exciting. Our baby is going to lie right here in her seat, and we are going to bring her home. I can hardly believe it's real.

The diaper bag contains a crocheted yellow outfit made by a friend, burp cloths, bottles, and other tiny baby things. I place the diaper bag on my lap. As we drive, I inhale the scent of roses and baby powder from the bag.

Steve and I sail downtown, jump out of the car, and race up the stairs to the placement office. Each step is the timeclock ticking in sync with my heartbeat.

We are greeted by Sister Barbara and our social worker.

We sit straight in wooden chairs as Sister Barbara fills us in. "Let me give you some background before the birth parents, Don and Krissy, show up. They should be here in about twenty minutes. They have been meeting with me weekly since Krissy was seven months pregnant. They were high school sweethearts who have been together three years, and Krissy is nineteen."

I ask, "How old is the baby?"

Sister answers, "She is five-and-a-half weeks old."

I lock eyes with Steve. I can tell by his face that he, too, is wondering what happened between the birth of the baby and now.

Looking at our expressions, Sister Barbara says, "So . . . initially, the birth parents chose you two to be the adoptive parents. But after the birth, Krissy felt torn about what to do. Her mother wanted her to keep the baby, while the birth father wanted to follow through with adoption."

I am on the edge of my seat in this cliffhanger scene, and I can't wait to hear the whole story. I press my hands down on my lap.

Sister Barbara continues. "Krissy kept the baby for two weeks, unsure what to do. Then, they put her in foster care, which is a service we provide, while they made up their minds. After three weeks, the birth parents decided to follow through with adoption."

I cringe thinking about how much this poor baby has been through, being passed around, wondering who Mom is. How can they do this to her? She is looking to attach, looking for safety, and these adults have jostled her around for weeks. How many faces does she need to look into until she finds one who will stay? I twist sideways in my seat.

Steve notices my discomfort and squeezes my hand in reassurance. With his gentle touch, I feel a settling in my heart and a strength in my soul. I straighten my back as a protective urge comes over me, and I know we will now become her forever family.

"After you meet the birth parents and the baby, the foster mother will fill you in on feeding, medication, and other details."

I nod, tighten my grip on my purse and glance behind me at the white front door, where the birth parents will soon appear and change our lives.

Sister Barbara, who seems to notice everything, smiles.

"Don't worry. You two will be fine. Just wait here. The birth parents will arrive shortly." She gestures for us to stand, walk toward the door, and wait about ten feet away from it.

Now, it seems like we are on stage in the dark, and a spotlight shines on the front door. Butterflies fill my belly, flying in chaotic circles. My feet are glued to the spot like there is an X taped on the floor and I am not allowed to move off my mark. Sister Barbara and the social worker stand behind us.

I whisper to Steve, "They will come toward us, right?"

Steve whispers, "I think so."

The ticking of the wall clock fills the room.

The door opens slowly.

In walks Krissy, a teary, nineteen-year-old blond in a cream-colored wool skirt and pink cashmere sweater. She dabs her reddened eyes with a crumpled tissue as she cradles a dark-haired sleeping bundle. Don, her tall, brown-haired boyfriend, keeps his eyes on Krissy. His arm rests protectively around her shoulder as he whispers words of comfort. They are so beautiful and mesmerizing in their own little world that is about to change forever too.

After a moment, Krissy looks at me, her eyes full of pain.

I memorize her face—her watery blue eyes, her quivering lips, her fair skin blushed from crying.

My daughter will look like her.

I feel a wave of love for her. She is about to give away her heart. Krissy moves closer to me until we are shoulder to shoulder. My arms ache to hold my daughter.

Shaken and trembling, Krissy looks up from her baby and whispers, "So you can't really have a child of your own, right?"

I feel an urge to drop my head in shame, picturing my empty womb. But I keep my head up. "No, I can't."

She sighs and appears a bit more settled, peering at her baby. I look at her, shuddering with nervous excitement.

With unsure arms, Krissy hands me her baby.

I am dropped into a world where all I can see is this twelve-pound jewel asleep in a pink blanket. Delicate eyelashes, rosebud lips, wisps of dark hair. A beauty. "What did you name her?"

Krissy tells me what they named the baby, and I tell her we will keep that name as a middle name and give her the name we picked.

The front door opens again, and this time a petite, middle-aged woman enters. Sister Barbara guides us to a couch.

Steve and I sit as Sister makes the introductions. "This is Mrs. Frank. She was the baby's foster parent for two weeks when the baby was three-to-five weeks old." Mrs. Frank leans forward and greets me with a warm smile. "She is a beautiful, strong baby who was over nine pounds at birth. I have loved caring for her." She shuffles through her handwritten notes. "She does have colic and was having seizures, so the doctor has her on anti-seizure medications."

I hold the sleeping baby tighter in my arms as worry creeps in. "What do you mean?"

"Poor thing. She was miserable. She wailed all day long. It was horrible to watch, so I called the doctor."

I look at the baby. So much upheaval for one little soul. She had birth parents for two weeks, then a foster mother for three weeks. So much separation. And seizures as well? It hits me that all the separation might have contributed to these seizures. My mind drifts off to think about this.

It bothers me that there is so little understanding about adoptee trauma. I have been studying attachment theory. Infants are totally vulnerable and instinctively seek a caretaker for safety and protection. The nervous system is wired for alarm, and as a defense mechanism, it chooses fight or flight when in danger. Too much time in danger produces excess cortisol, which stresses the body, making relaxation and digestion difficult.

Seizures could be an expression of an over-stressed nervous system. This poor baby! I grit my teeth and shake my head to return to listening.

Mrs. Frank pulls out a small stack of papers with detailed notes about feedings, sleep patterns, health issues, and medications. I blink at the many pencil marks on the papers. I listen intently, nodding and trying to take it all in, while twinges of anger and sadness prick me. This baby has had to manage too much, too young.

And jolts of happiness remind me I am here to love and protect her now.

After a few minutes, Mrs. Frank hands me her stack.

These papers are about to become my new bible. These are the instructions, the directives, the methods to feed and handle our new baby. I turn them over. I will memorize them.

But the moment is bigger than schedules and formulas. I sense God in the room, smiling as a witness to what He promised me: "You will receive."

And here she is, a beautiful being He has placed in my arms for safekeeping. Our love for her will be immense.

God is smiling like a warm grandfather in the corner, saying, "I trust you three to go forth with My love."

I settle into a realistic acceptance of what is, a new person in our lives who has already experienced trauma, another person, imperfect like us, whom we will shield and love with all the human might we can muster.

Sister Barbara nods at the birth parents, who are huddled together by the desk. She leans over, gently lifts the still sleeping baby from my arms, and whispers, "It's time for the birth parents to leave, and they want a brief moment."

I am pulled out of my God-filled reverie and watch Sister Barbara hand the baby to Don and Krissy, who walk to the farthest corner of the room to privately say goodbye to their birth daughter.

Don puts his arm around Krissy and holds her close as they create a tight circle. They bow their heads as they whisper their final words. Krissy wipes away tears.

It seems too private to watch, so I turn away out of respect for the three of them. My heart hurts for them, and my eyes water. When they return, we all stand.

With resolve, Don takes the baby from Krissy. As he hands the baby to Steve, he whispers to his birth daughter, "This is your father."

Steve envelops the pink bundle in his arms and stares at her round angelic face.

In a moment that seems magical, the baby, who has slept through every second thus far, opens her eyes for the first time and looks right into Steve's eyes.

He gasps as tears form while he stares at his new daughter.

The open placement felt like it had all been about the adults and our emotions. But the instant she looked up at Steve, a crater blew a hole into the earth as we knew it.

Her presence fills the room. She is a fragile yet powerful whole person. My heart dives into the blue swirl of her eyes, and I want to swim here forever. I feel love, a touch of fear, and the thrill of God's miracle.

God grabs me by the collar when I run too fast. He tells me to slow down and reminds me I won't be left behind. He plunks me into a boat and promises what I keep forgetting—that, in the end, I will get what I desire if I have humility and if I can trust the river to flow at its own pace.

Chapter Thirty

CLOWN CAR

Four Months Later, November 1986

THE DOORBELL RINGS the night before our daughter's christening. My parents have arrived early, and we are waiting for the rest of the family to show up at my house.

Dad follows me as I open the door. He says, "They better be ringing the doorbell with their elbows."

This is one of his corny Dad jokes that I love, and I play my role.

"Why?" I ask.

"Because they better have their hands full with gifts and food."

I giggle. As soon as I open the front door, all eleven of my siblings pile into our small condo.

My dad counts people as they come in, saying to each, "You're back in the will."

This is another Dad saying. Each year when any of us called to wish Dad a happy birthday, he would say, "You're back in the will." It was a fun joke made even funnier because, with twelve kids, there wasn't much to go around except for a legacy of unconditional love, in which he was always wealthy.

His love has made us all rich.

There are so many people coming through the door that I have almost forgotten how many of us there are when we all get together. I start to laugh. They look like clowns emerging from a clown car, towing colorful gift bags and cute children.

My brother Kevin pats Steve on the back as he passes. "How's it feel to be a new dad?"

As Steve helps with the luggage and sleeping bags, tears form in his eyes, and he tells Kevin, "I feel elated. I feel apprehensive. I hope I'm going to be a good father."

My sisters Maria and Cefe crane their necks, asking, "Where's the baby? How is she doing?"

"Oh, the baby is sleeping right now," I say. "She finally got over her colic and can digest formula better."

Maria hands me a soft brown teddy bear with a pink bow, and I put it on the table with the other gifts.

"Awww . . . This is a cute bear."

Cefe smiles. "You must be so relieved. I can't wait to meet her."

The noise level rises as seventeen people laugh and chat with the trill of a tree full of birds. The house swells like a stuffed turkey as Kenny and Rick look for a spare spot on the rug to plop down their bags.

Ken turns on the TV. "The Forty-Niners better win today."

Bonny drops her sleeping bag near all the others and rushes to the kitchen to help Mom, who is chopping vegetables for dinner.

The volume grows louder from multiple conversations going on at once.

I overhear Peggy ask, "Did everyone remember to bring something pink to wear for the baptism tomorrow?"

As I set the table, I perk up my ears to hear Anita and Josefa sing, "Child of Mine." This is my favorite new song; they know it and must have memorized it to sing to us. My smile is as wide as the sky.

Soon the smell of arroz con pollo wafts through the air.

Mom's eyes twinkle as she quietly observes her whole family in one place. She calls out, "Dinnertime!"

Steve enters, carrying a bench from the neighbors, and sets it down at our small dining room table. My brother, Sean, follows with a second bench, and everyone scrambles to find a seat.

We sit shoulder to shoulder like we did as children, while mom brings the food to the table: a large casserole, a big green salad, a jug of water, and an open bottle of white wine.

When most everyone is seated, Peter laughs. "We are squeezed in here like rats in a cheesebox."

We chuckle. I'm getting all the vibes of being back at home as a kid, cozy from the warmth of a big family. I had kind of forgotten this world, having been lost for two years on my road to motherhood. It's all coming back to me now.

Kevin sits next to me, just like he used to when we were younger. I still see him as that younger brother, the eight-year-old with dirty hands and a crew cut. I joke, "Kevin! Did you wash your hands?"

He hits me on the shoulder as we smile in our nostalgia.

Dad looks around and notices that Ken and Rick are not at the table. He stands up, cups his hands like a megaphone, and pretends to be a priest. "Pray for those who are not here."

Ken and Rick rush to the table and squeeze onto the already-packed benches. Dad smiles as he takes in the sight of the whole crew. My mother lights up too. It's as if they like it best when we are all together.

In a more serious manner, Dad bows his head and folds his hands in prayer. "Bless us, O Lord, and these thy gifts, which we are about to receive from thy bounty through Christ our Lord. Amen. God bless Kenny, Peggy, Bonny, Susy, Sean, Cefe, Maria, Josefa, Kevin, Peter, Anita, Ricky." Dad looks at me and Steve. He winks at us. "And the new baby."

Tears fill my eyes, and I press my lips together. I am surprised when Steve stands up because he is usually introverted, but he feels compelled to speak.

"Thank you all for coming. Some of you guys packed into a few cars and drove eight hours. It means so much that you are with us to welcome our child into the family."

Soon, the sound of clinking silverware meshes with raucous laughter and fussing over the little ones.

Mom, who is still in her apron, goes back to the kitchen to get bread.

Sean calls out, "Mom, join us at the table."

As I look around at this huge, amazing group, a calm familiarity comes over me, and a loss of self-consciousness sets in. I am one of the gang, back home again.

Then, a high-pitched cry from upstairs hushes us all.

Peggy gasps, "Oh, it's the baby!"

Bonny says, "Go get her. We want to see her!"

I feel a warm buzz. Our baby is going to meet her big family.

I zip up the stairs and walk to her crib, speaking in soft tones. "Hey, my pretty little girl. How did you sleep?"

I grab a clean onesie and a little yellow dress. "Do you hear noise downstairs? The house is full of family who want to meet you. Everybody is here—your grandma and grandpa and all your aunts and uncles. Let's go meet them."

I use a tiny pink brush to smooth her tufts of hair, and I lift her gently into my arms. With joy in my step, I make my way down the stairs. As I bring her toward the group, all eyes focus on her.

I sit with her in the lounge chair as the family crowds around to meet the little queen.

My three-year-old nephew, who is holding a glowworm toy, peers closely at the baby's round face and big eyes and says in his high, nasally voice, "She looks like a bug or something."

We all laugh. Next, his wavy-haired, one-year-old sister with a bottle dangling from her mouth comes over and places one chubby little finger on the baby's forehead.

I lean in. "These are your cousins, Trenton and Shahera."

Mom leans over, smooths the baby's blanket, and whispers to me, "You look right at home."

———

That night, my siblings do what we always did at my parents' house during big family visits when it came time to sleep and the bedrooms were full. They unroll sleeping bags that cover the entire living room floor of our small condo.

In the morning, I creep down the stairs and look at the living room carpeted with family. Not one square inch of the actual rug can be seen. My mother is already in the kitchen making coffee, and she and I giggle as I tiptoe to avoid stepping on the snoring mounds.

Mom raises her eyebrows and says, "You aren't used to the big group anymore, are you?"

I shake my head. "Nope."

Once I get into the kitchen, Mom smiles at me with bright eyes, holds my gaze, and points to a corner.

I turn and see a little girl's wicker chair with a red bow on it.

No! It can't be.

When Cefe gave birth to Shahera a year ago, Mom gave Cefe a wicker chair, the one she had told me and Cefe she was saving for her first granddaughter. So this can't be that one.

I look closer. This one has different colors than the first one. This one has colors for *my* baby, my *perfect* baby girl. I touch the pink-and-yellow painted flowers along the glossy wood frame. On the seat back, painted in blue and pink, is my daughter's name.

Epilogue

Twenty-One Years Later

DOCTORS AND NURSES rush in and out of the hospital room, unsure why my daughter can't deliver her baby. She has been in severe pain for six hours, in labor for twelve. I am beyond frustrated. I can't stand to see her suffer. Why don't the doctors know what's wrong? Why can't they fix it?

Another hour passes, and a new doctor arrives as Steve and I are ushered into the hallway. A half hour later, he comes out and tells us that the baby is face up, which means it will have a difficult, and possibly dangerous, time making its way through the pelvis.

"What are you going to do?" I ask.

"She needs a C-section," the doctor says, "and she needs it now."

I watch helplessly as our daughter is whisked away to an operating room.

We wait. On pins and needles. I try not to look at any clocks. I pray to God, "Please watch over my baby girl and her baby boy."

Thirty minutes later, I am standing anxiously against the wall in the hospital corridor when the operating doors finally open.

As staff wheel her past us in the hallway, our daughter's face is flushed, and she is holding her newborn son. Her eyes are filled with awe as she stares at his reddish face and places her index finger in his tiny hand.

We gingerly walk behind them but at a distance so my daughter and her husband can bond with the newborn. Just outside of our daughter's room in the maternity ward, I press my shoulder into Steve's as we lean against the wall.

Is she okay? Is the baby okay? My heart is beating out of my chest.

A nurse comes into the hall, and I stop her. "How are they?" I ask.

"Mother and baby are doing well."

I exhale, and Steve and I enter the room.

A nurse gently hands my grandson to his father, my son-in-law, who smiles broadly as the nurse teaches him how to swaddle the baby.

After a few minutes, Steve gets to hold the baby. His eyes sparkle, and he tears up.

My arms ache to reach just like when I first saw my daughter as a baby. And yet, I am tentative.

I look at her wistfully, smiling, and she says, "Let my mom hold the baby."

I blink back tears. Steve hands me our new grandson.

As the weight of his little body sinks into my arms, my journey washes over me: the times I was wheeled into, and out of, operating rooms in a hospital like this with Steve by my side; the physical and emotional toll of infertility and ectopic pregnancies; the up-and-down dance of grief and hope; the slowing down and trusting in God's presence; our challenging adoption voyage; my dream of motherhood fulfilled.

And now, my daughter's dream has come true. My grandson turns his face toward the soft sound of his mother's voice.

I inhale and sigh. The top of his fuzzy head smells like new, and I close my eyes to prolong this precious experience.

The world stops for a minute, and a sense of peace settles in me as I hold this beautiful life.

Motherhood doesn't always happen as planned. But as my grandson slowly opens his eyes, the music of God's plan fills the room and brings me home.

Acknowledgments

It takes a village; it takes a family; it takes a community—of friends and mostly professionals—to make a book. The book is like Cinderella's old drabby dress and apron sooty and gray from the hearth, all dusted off and washed and pressed and pinned and snipped and sewed to a thing of sky-blue beauty by little birds and friendly mice.

I want to thank the team from Acorn Publishing starting at the top with Holly Kammier with her keen eye and friendly smile, to Nico who managed all the pieces of colored thread in the garment, to the talented and incisive Leslie Ferguson, my content editor with the eyes of an eagle, keen on making the manuscript as bright and clear for the reader as possible. My heartfelt gratitude to Marni Freedman from IMWA, who has coached me through my first book in 2011, my second in 2018, my third in 2021, and finally this memoir. Her talent, patience, and loving spirit has been an anchor throughout all my writing whims. The writing community in San Diego is full of nice people and creative courses and events. Thank you to San Diego Writers Ink and the International Memoir Writers Association.

My heart smiles as I think of my siblings who always support whatever I write or paint, a legacy from our childhood where we teased each other but grew up with unconditional love from our parents. My longtime friends Carole, George, and Golda encourage my creativity. My husband Steve listens and moves around me like a quiet hawk—circling, dipping, and flying in a wide circle, helping me feel free to roam or free to fly or free to return to the nest and rest in his arms.

Finally, this tale is really about how I found the greatest gift from God in an unconventional way. And though neither of us had much control over how we found each other and ended up together, you, my dear daughter, are my heart and I thank you for the preciousness of your love in my life.

About the Author

Vincentia Schroeter grew up in a small town in central California as the fourth of twelve children. Intrigued by the many different personalities in her family, she knew by the age of sixteen that she wanted to be a counselor. She put herself through college and graduate school in order to pursue her dreams.

Vin is the author of the award-winning self-help book, *Communication Breakthrough: How Using Brain Science and Listening to Body Cues Can Change Your Relationships* (2018). She also co-authored a training manual on somatic psychotherapy that has been translated into three languages.

After a forty-year career as a psychotherapist listening to clients' stories of pain and trauma, Vin felt drawn to share her own story. She now lives in San Diego with her husband Steve and enjoys pickleball, painting, and time with family, including her dog, Ren.